Just What I Need!

Learning Experiences to Use on Multiple Days in Multiple Ways

BERTIE KINGORE
AUTHOR

Jeffery Kingore
GRAPHIC DESIGN

PROFESSIONAL ASSOCIATES PUBLISHING

Other Publications by
Bertie Kingore, Ph.D.

Alphabetters: Thinking Adventures with the Alphabet (TASK CARDS)
Assessment: Time Saving Procedures for Busy Teachers, 3rd ed.
Assessment Interactive CD-ROM
Bertie's Book Notes 2005
Centers in Minutes!
Centers in Minutes CD-ROM Vol. 1: Grades K-8
Centers in Minutes CD-ROM Vol. 2: Learners with Limited Reading and Writing Skills
Differentiation: Simplified, Realistic, and Effective
Differentiation Interactive CD-ROM
Engaging Creative Thinking: Activities to Integrate Creative Problem Solving
Integrating Thinking: Practical Strategies and Activities
Kingore Observation Inventory (KOI), 2nd ed.
Literature Celebrations: Catalysts to High-Level Book Responses, 2nd ed.
Reading Strategies for Advanced Primary Readers
Teaching without Nonsense: Activities to Encourage High-Level Responses
We Care: A Curriculum for Preschool-Kindergarten, 2nd ed.

FOR INFORMATION OR ORDERS, CONTACT:

PROFESSIONAL ASSOCIATES PUBLISHING
PO Box 28056
Austin, Texas 78755-8056
Toll free phone/fax: 866-335-1460

VISIT US ONLINE!
www.kingore.com

Just What I Need!
Strategies to Use in Multiple Ways on Multiple Days

Copyright © 2003 Bertie Kingore

Published by **PROFESSIONAL ASSOCIATES PUBLISHING**

Printed in the United States of America
ISBN: 0-9716233-2-5

Table of Contents

Introduction

Just What I Need! is a potpourri of simple-to-prepare learning experiences to incorporate on multiple days in multiple ways. During the development, expansion, and modeling of these activities in kindergarten through high school classes, teachers commented on the tasks' simplicity, effectiveness, and application to multiple contents. Use these tasks instead of the more simplistic, one-correct-answer assignments used in the past with which both students and teachers have grown weary.

THE FOLLOWING STRATEGIES REPRESENT THE FOCUS OF THIS BOOK.

Students as Producers

Every activity has a section inviting students to become producers. Students demonstrate higher levels of learning as producers creating their own models instead of consumers only responding to assignments. Because students generate examples, a wider variety of responses at different levels of understanding and complexity result than when teachers produce the problems or examples for students to answer.

Modeling for Success

Initially, these learning experiences are introduced through teacher-directed instruction. Students can not work independently when they are uncertain how to complete the work successfully. The activities must be modeled and the students experience success before students can proceed by themselves.

Flexible Grouping

The learning experiences can be completed as a whole class, but master teachers realize that whole-class instruction is more limited in its ability to meet individual learning needs and actively engage students. Therefore, these tasks are most effective when completed by small groups, pairs, or individuals.

Active Learning

Students who are mentally engaged are seldom bored; active involvement increases their learning and personal connections to the content. The goal is for most of the students to be actively engaged most of the time.

High-Level Thinking and Responses

High-level thinking is the right and need of every student. The open-ended nature of these tasks challenge students to analyze, synthesize, and evaluate.

Multiple Content and Topic Applications

These techniques and activities are adaptable to multiple situations and topics of study and are easily used with a minimum of teacher preparation. Teachers report that they use these activities several times a year in different units of study.

Kingore, B. (2003). Just What I Need! Austin: Professional Associates Publishing.

Cube a Thought

PURPOSES

- To integrate high-level thinking into class discussions
- To enable teachers to assess students' depth and complexity of information
- To increase students' active involvement and mental engagement
- To engage kinesthetic and visual learners
- To develop students' questioning skills

GRADE LEVELS: 1 - 12

DESCRIPTION

Cube a Thought is a technique that requires students to apply thinking skills and inquiry to multiple content areas and topics. Instead of developing multiple questions and learning experiences for every class discussion, teachers and students use the provided patterns to fold and tape together several copies of a cube that corresponds to the instructional objectives. Provide one cube for each small group during a class discussion. A group member gently rolls the cube to determine how that group is to respond. The prompt that ends up on the top of the cube determines the question or learning task for students to complete.

To increase students' motivation and choices, allow groups to roll the cube twice and then decide between the two options. A group size of two or three works best so all students have opportunities to roll the cube.

Use the blank cube patterns to create additional prompts that relate to students' instructional needs. For example, write supplementary question prompts on each cube surface that apply to the specific topic being studied.

Action Responses. Students work in groups. After rolling the cube provided on page 8, each group has two or three minutes to prepare what they think is the best response to the prompt on the top of the cube. They then perform their responses for the class.

Thinking Skills, Vocabulary, Fiction, Nonfiction, Math, and Science Responses. Students roll one of the cubes on pages 7 to 12, apply the prompt to the content being studied, and share their responses.

Kingore, B. (2003). <u>Just What I Need</u>! Austin: Professional Associates Publishing.

Questioning Skills.
* Students roll the question cube on page 6 or one of the thinking-skills cubes on pages 7 to 8 and use the prompt to poses a question for others.
* Each group works together to pose one question about the topic or story for each side of the cube. Later, groups exchange questions to answer.

Writing Responses. Copy the cube on page 12 or use a blank cube to outline the parts of a different writing task. As the teacher facilitates the whole group, individuals use this cube to signal the part of their composition on which they are working. The question mark signals a need for help or clarification. After each student completes the first draft, provide another copy of the cube on colored paper. Students use the colored cube to signal which section of their work they are rewriting or editing.

STUDENTS AS PRODUCERS

Students are producers throughout the multiple applications of Cube a Thought. They produce original responses, pose questions, and answer each other's prompts based upon which cube they are using.

The large, blank cube pattern is an appropriate size on which most students can write and/or illustrate. Instead of taping the cube, students can use circular, peel-off stickers to hold the cube together. The circles allow the cube to be reopened so information can be listed on the outside of the cube and answers posted on the inside. The following are suggested student applications.

Book Response Variations.
* Students write and illustrate one literary element of a specific story or novel on each cube surface and write the title and author of the book inside.
* When focusing on sequence, students write five key events in sequence. They write the main idea on the sixth side and the title and author inside.
* Encourage advanced students to incorporate symbols for the characters or key events instead of using more literal illustrations.

Me Cube. In each section, children draw or write something about themselves or things they like. Children later share their cubes with the class.

Phonics. In each section, students paste on, draw, and/or label pictures that incorporate the sound being studied.

Topic Questions. On each surface of the large, blank cube, students pose and write a question to ask others about the topic or story. It may require more analysis to pose applicable questions than to only answer questions.

Topic Organizer. On each surface, students write a significant fact or attribute relating to the topic.

Oral Report. Instead of note cards, students organize the main points of their report on a cube to demonstrate as they share their information.

Kingore, B. (2003). Just What I Need! Austin: Professional Associates Publishing.

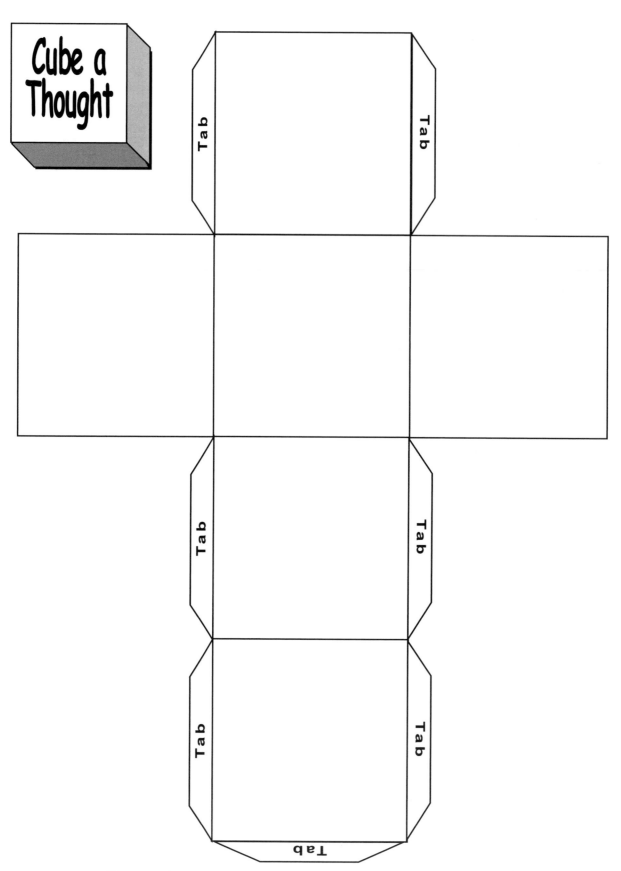

Cube a Thought

Tab

Tab

Tab

Tab

Tab

Tab

Tab

Kingore, B. (2003). <u>Just What I Need</u>! Austin: Professional Associates Publishing.

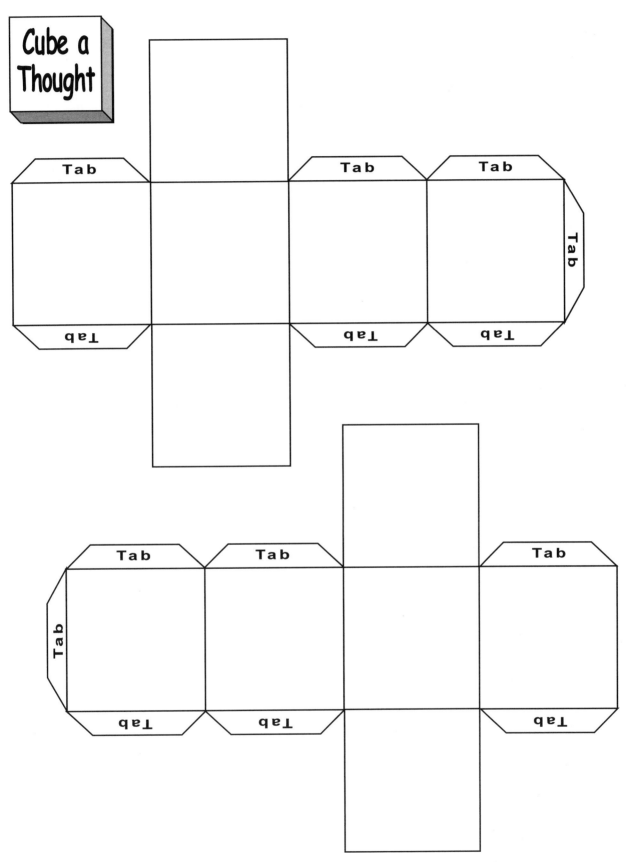

Question Words

Students roll the Question Words cube and then plan a question to ask others that begins with that word.

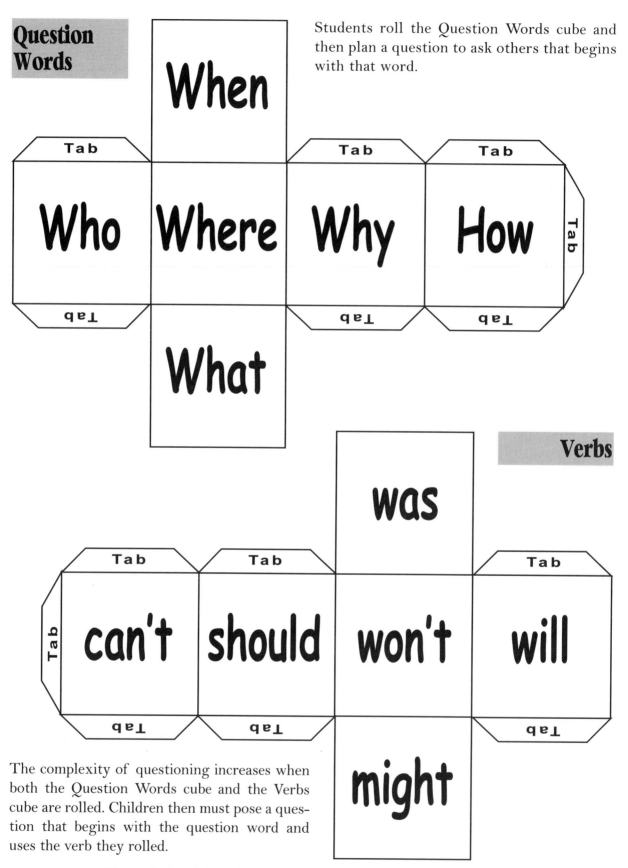

When

Tab

Who | Where | Why | How

Tab

What

Verbs

was

Tab | Tab | Tab

can't | should | won't | will

might

The complexity of questioning increases when both the Question Words cube and the Verbs cube are rolled. Children then must pose a question that begins with the question word and uses the verb they rolled.

Kingore, B. (2003). <u>Just What I Need</u>! Austin: Professional Associates Publishing.

Thinking Skills:
Knowledge &
Comprehension

Students roll one of the three cubes organized by Bloom's Taxonomy of Thinking Skills. They then respond to that prompt.

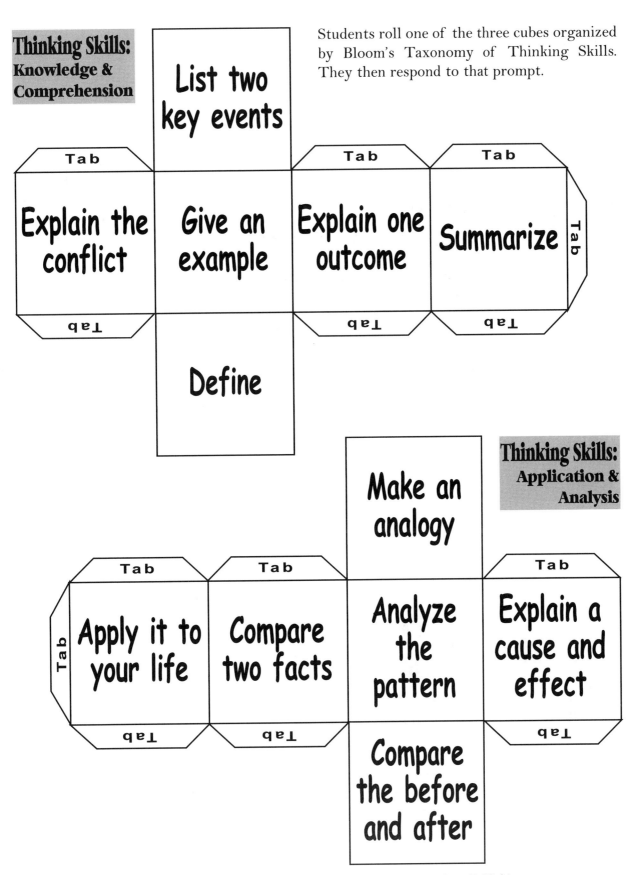

List two
key events

Tab

Tab

Tab

Explain the
conflict

Give an
example

Explain one
outcome

Summarize

Tab

Tab

Tab

Tab

Define

Thinking Skills:
Application &
Analysis

Make an
analogy

Tab

Tab

Tab

Apply it to
your life

Compare
two facts

Analyze
the
pattern

Explain a
cause and
effect

Tab

Tab

Tab

Tab

Compare
the before
and after

Kingore, B. (2003). Just What I Need! Austin: Professional Associates Publishing.

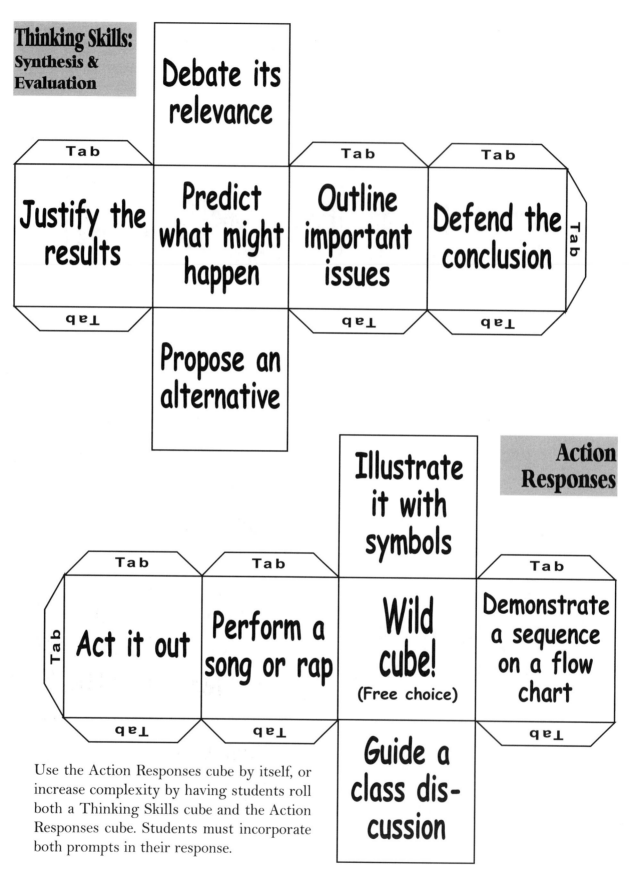

Thinking Skills:
Synthesis &
Evaluation

Debate its
relevance

Tab

Justify the
results

Predict
what might
happen

Outline
important
issues

Tab

Defend the
conclusion

Tab

Tab

Tab

Tab

Propose an
alternative

Illustrate
it with
symbols

**Action
Responses**

Tab

Tab

Tab

Tab

Act it out

Perform a
song or rap

Wild
cube!
(Free choice)

Demonstrate
a sequence
on a flow
chart

Tab

Tab

Tab

Guide a
class dis-
cussion

Use the Action Responses cube by itself, or
increase complexity by having students roll
both a Thinking Skills cube and the Action
Responses cube. Students must incorporate
both prompts in their response.

Kingore, B. (2003). <u>Just What I Need</u>! Austin: Professional Associates Publishing.

Nonfiction

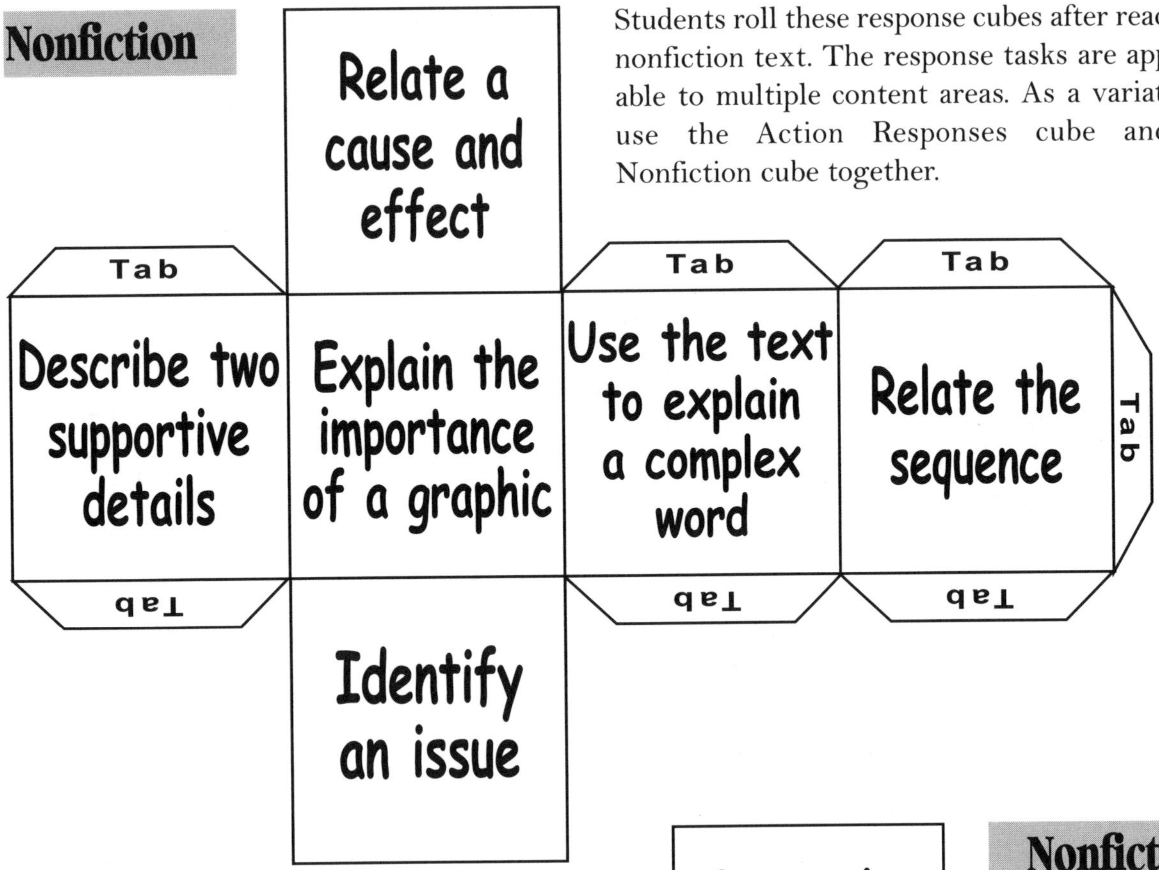

Relate a
cause and
effect

Students roll these response cubes after reading nonfiction text. The response tasks are applicable to multiple content areas. As a variation, use the Action Responses cube and a Nonfiction cube together.

Tab

Describe two
supportive
details

Explain the
importance
of a graphic

Use the text
to explain
a complex
word

Relate the
sequence

Tab

Tab

Tab

Tab

Tab

Identify
an issue

Summarize
the
content

Nonfiction

Tab

Tab

Tab

Tab

Relate
this to
your life

Compare
similarities
and
differences

Predict a
probable
future
outcome

Explain one
resource

Tab

Tab

Tab

Identify
two key
facts

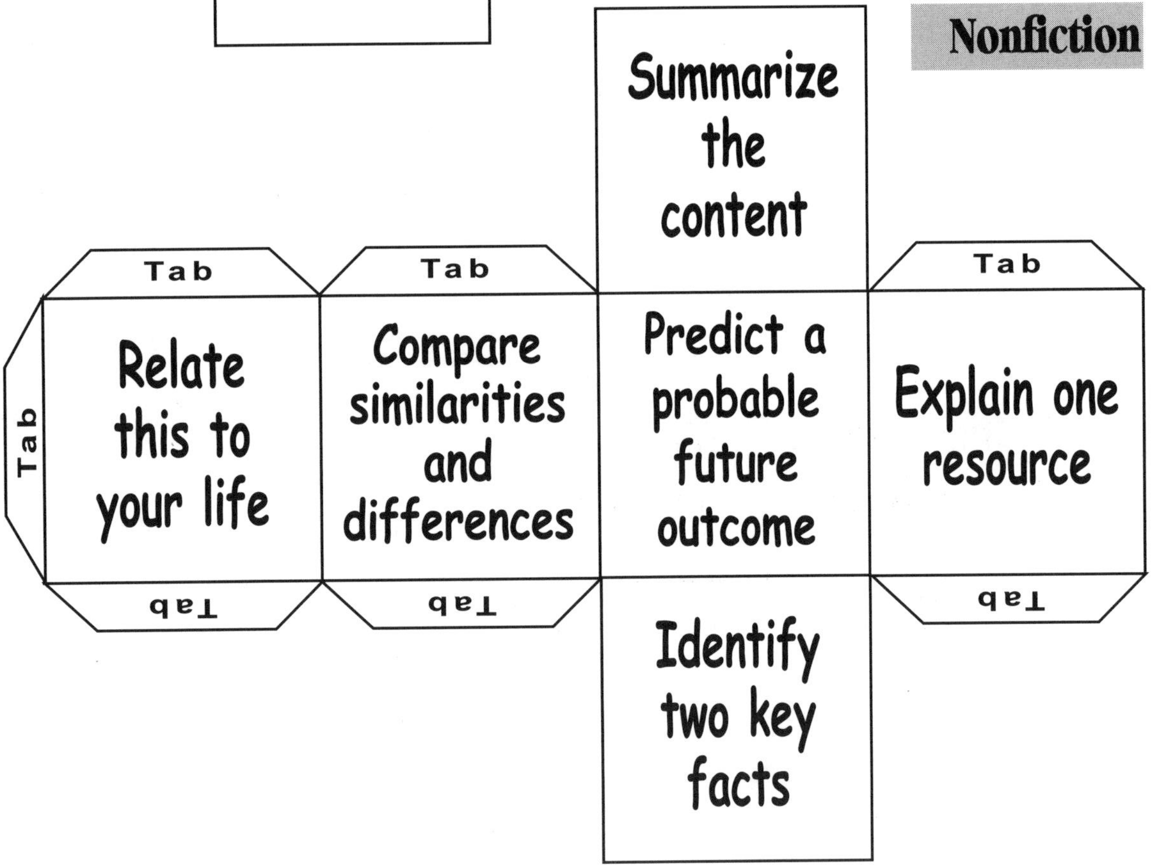

Kingore, B. (2003). Just What I Need! Austin: Professional Associates Publishing.

Fiction

Students roll these fiction response cubes after reading a picture book or novel. As a variation, use the Action Responses cube and a Fiction cube together.

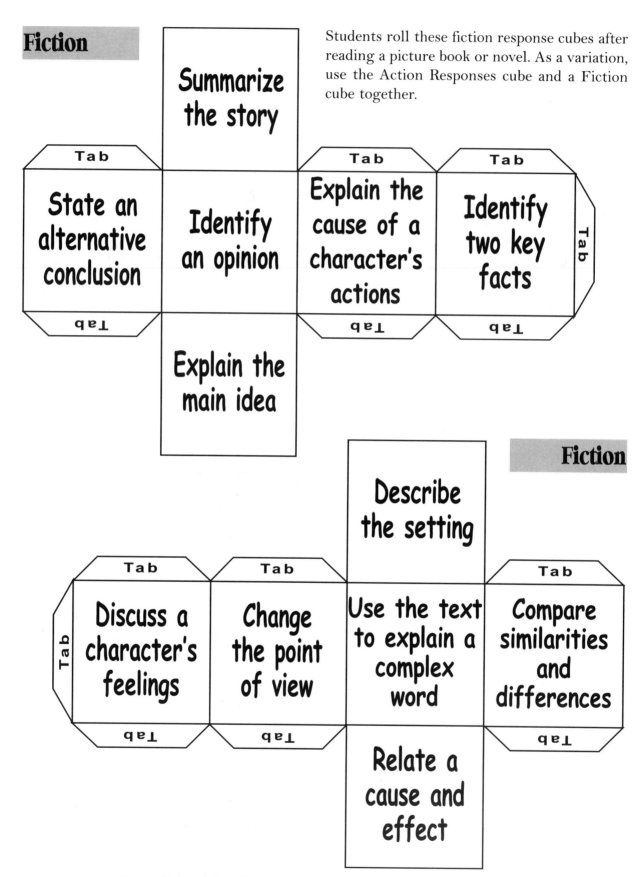

Summarize the story

Tab

State an alternative conclusion

Identify an opinion

Explain the cause of a character's actions

Identify two key facts

Tab

Tab

Tab

Tab

Tab

Tab

Explain the main idea

Fiction

Describe the setting

Tab

Tab

Tab

Tab

Discuss a character's feelings

Change the point of view

Use the text to explain a complex word

Compare similarities and differences

Tab

Tab

Tab

Relate a cause and effect

Kingore, B. (2003). <u>Just What I Need</u>! Austin: Professional Associates Publishing.

Math

These math responses require students to analyze math problems. As an example, write a long division problem on the board. Groups roll the cube and respond accordingly.

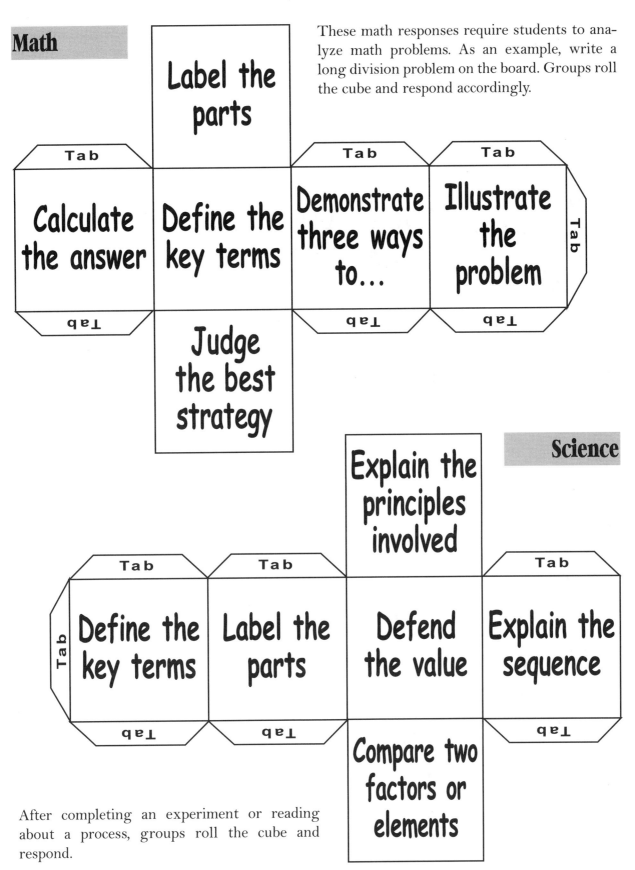

Label the parts

Tab

Calculate the answer | Define the key terms | Demonstrate three ways to… | Illustrate the problem

Tab

Judge the best strategy

Science

Explain the principles involved

Tab | Tab | Tab

Define the key terms | Label the parts | Defend the value | Explain the sequence

Tab

Compare two factors or elements

After completing an experiment or reading about a process, groups roll the cube and respond.

Kingore, B. (2003). Just What I Need! Austin: Professional Associates Publishing.

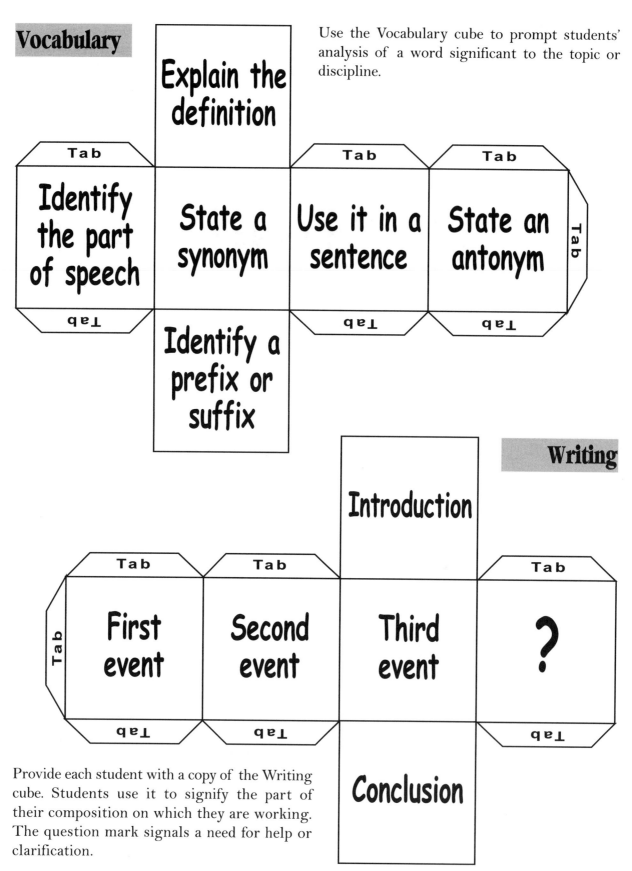

Vocabulary

Explain the definition

Tab

Identify the part of speech

Tab

State a synonym

Use it in a sentence

Tab

State an antonym

Tab

Tab

Identify a prefix or suffix

Use the Vocabulary cube to prompt students' analysis of a word significant to the topic or discipline.

Writing

Introduction

Tab

Tab

Tab

Tab

First event

Second event

Third event

?

Tab

Tab

Tab

Conclusion

Provide each student with a copy of the Writing cube. Students use it to signify the part of their composition on which they are working. The question mark signals a need for help or clarification.

Kingore, B. (2003). <u>Just What I Need</u>! Austin: Professional Associates Publishing.

Interactive Questioning

PURPOSES

- To review and synthesize information
- To integrate high-level thinking into class discussions
- To enable teachers to encourage and assess students' depth and complexity of information
- To increase students' active involvement
- To develop students' questioning skills

GRADE LEVELS: 2 - 12

DESCRIPTION

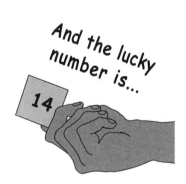

And the lucky number is...

The interactive questioning technique randomly selects students to pose and answer questions. Copy and cut apart the number cards on page 15, and place them in a container to randomly select the group to respond.

Interactive questioning requires students to apply high-level thinking and inquiry skills as they become actively involved in the information related to a current topic of study. Instead of teachers developing multiple questions to guide every class discussion, teachers facilitate the students' review of the significant information as students pose questions and respond to classmates' questions. The random nature of the technique adds to the appeal of the activity.

PROCEDURE

1. Arrange the class into groups of three to four students. Then, assign each group a number.

2. Provide three to five minutes for each group to plan, discuss, and write two questions to ask another group about the content. The groups are invited to use their text materials and notes to review and determine the most significant information. Requiring groups to develop two questions encourages more review of the content and decreases the likelihood that another group will pose the same questions.

Kingore, B. (2003). Just What I Need! Austin: Professional Associates Publishing.

NOTES

3. Draw a number card to select the questioning group. That group states one of their questions for the others to answer.

4. Provide a think time of two to three minutes.
    a. Each group discusses and writes out their answer or key ideas.
    b. The questioning group writes out the key components they expect in the answer. (Requiring the questioning group to write components keeps them actively engaged in the task.)

5. Use the number cards to randomly select the group that is to answer the question. That group addresses their answer to the questioning group who responds with their satisfaction or concerns regarding the answer. (Selecting the answering group after think time encourages all groups to discuss and prepare instead of engaging in off-task behaviors.)

6. Replace the used number cards back in the container and shuffle before proceeding with the next question. (Remixing all the numbers requires the continued participation of every group.)

Students often raise the possibility of the same group being selected disproportionately. Address probability; this process presents an authentic probability problem for some student to research as the technique is used.

Interactive questioning typically produces more questions than can be used in one setting. Return to the activity another day if the interest merits further interaction.

The questions are frequently well developed and quite strong in their use of content. Consider other ways in which the groups' questions can be used.
*   Post the questions for the groups to review and compare.
*   Use the questions on a test. The students are delighted that they already know some of the questions.
*   Replace homework assignments with the student-posed questions. Students feel more ownership and interest in a homework task when it involves their questions.
*   Use the questions as tasks in learning centers.

To maximize the value of interactive questioning, some groups may need a more concrete stimulus for how to pose thoughtful questions instead of only simple detail questions. Brainstorm as a class, and list examples of high-level questions. If preferred, provide a paper copy of high-level question prompts for these groups to skim and incorporate.

Kingore, B. (2003). <u>Just What I Need</u>! Austin: Professional Associates Publishing.

STUDENTS AS PRODUCERS

Students are producers throughout the process of using interactive questioning. They pose original questions and answer each other's prompts based upon their review and synthesis of the content being studied.

1	2	3	4
5	6	7	8
9	10	11	12
13	14	15	16
17	18	19	20

Kingore, B. (2003). <u>Just What I Need</u>! Austin: Professional Associates Publishing.

KWL Variations

PURPOSES

- To review, organize, and synthesize information
- To serve as springboards for discussing, researching, or writing more extensively about topics
- To encourage and assess students' depth and complexity of information
- To encourage students to list resources as they acquire and organize information

GRADE LEVELS: 1-12

DESCRIPTION

KWL (Ogle, 1986) is a popular strategy designed to activate a child's prior knowledge, help formulate purpose-setting questions, and assess comprehension. A KWL chart consists of three areas labeled: *What I Know, What I Want to Know,* and *What I Learned.* Initially completed as a teacher-directed activity, children brainstorm what they already know about the topic as the teacher writes this information in the first section of the chart. Next, the teacher asks the children what they want to learn about the topic and records that information in the second section. As the class reads and learns about the topic, the teacher and the children fill in the third section. This strategy becomes a concrete way to demonstrate the new information the children are learning. Eventually, students assume increased responsibility for completing the chart.

VARIATIONS

Rows. Design the KWL form as rows instead of columns. This change better suites young students' handwriting.

Graphic. For visual appeal, design the KWL as a three-part graphic. One example is included on page 18. Ideally, incorporate KWL graphics that correspond to topics and units, such as three instruments used in meteorology.

KWLS. Add a fourth row labeled *What I Still Want to Learn* (see page 19). This addition clarifies that everything about most topics is not learned through one investigation.

Kingore, B. (2003). <u>Just What I Need</u>! Austin: Professional Associates Publishing.

STUDENTS AS PRODUCERS

Encourage small groups and then individuals to complete KWL and KWL variations without direct teacher instruction. These responses increase ownership in the task and allow for greater variations in the levels of the responses.

Research. Individuals complete *K* and *W* sections and then circle one or more items in the *W* section to focus on in their research. This process helps students narrow their research topic.

KWRDL. Individuals add *R* and *D* sections for *Resources I Can Use* and *What I Will Do to Learn* (see page 20). These additions encourage students to consider available resource options and develop an action plan to organize their learning.

Bulletin Board. Design KWL or one of its variations as a bulletin board. Students use index cards or index-sized sticky notes to post responses in each appropriate section. The bulletin board might be used for one topic or become a year-around board that focuses background and learning for every topic or unit.

Kingore, B. (2003). <u>Just What I Need</u>! Austin: Professional Associates Publishing.

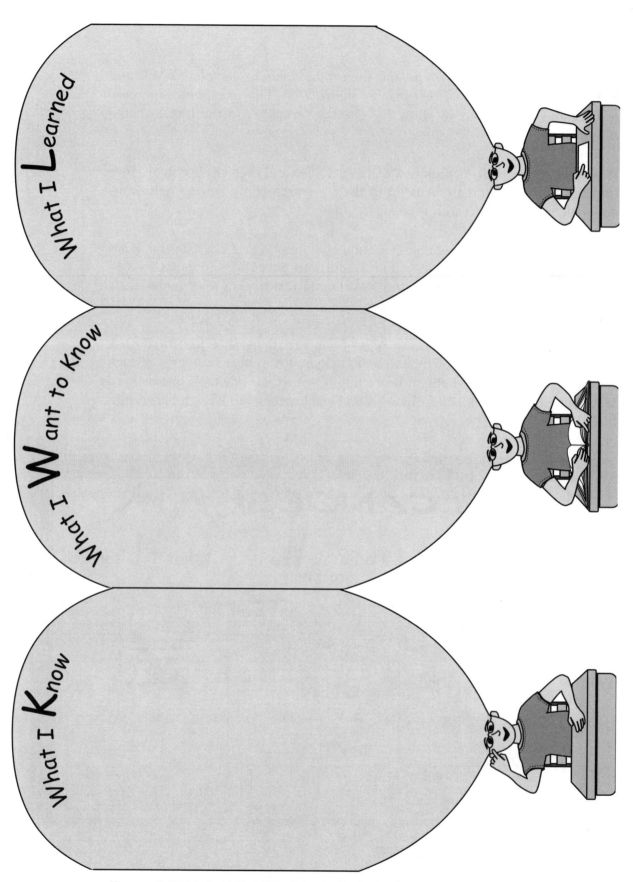

Kingore, B. (2003). <u>Just What I Need</u>! Austin: Professional Associates Publishing.

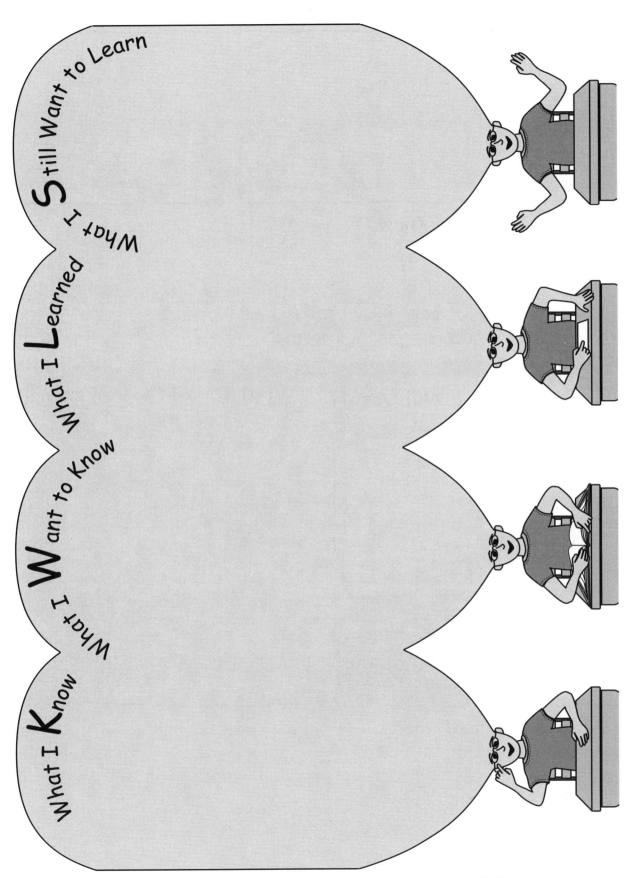

What I **K**now   What I **W**ant to Know   What I **L**earned   What I **S**till Want to Learn

Kingore, B. (2003). <u>Just What I Need</u>! Austin: Professional Associates Publishing.

What I **K**now

What I **W**ant to Know

Resources I Will Use

What I Will **D**o to Learn

1.

2.

3.

4.

What I **L**earned

Question Chart

PURPOSES

- To integrate high-level thinking into class discussions
- To develop students' questioning skills
- To increase students' active involvement
- To assess students' integration and transfer of skills
- To encourage students to analyze the most significant attributes or concepts of a topic

GRADE LEVELS: K - 6

DESCRIPTION

A Question Chart is a simple and effective technique to encourage students' questioning skills and recognize their involvement in classroom discussions. Instead of teachers needing to develop multiple questions to guide every class discussion, teachers facilitate the students' review of the significant information as students pose questions and respond to class-mates' questions.

Make an overhead transparency of page 23, or use a piece of colored poster board and copies of the chart pieces on page 24 to produce a large chart. (Laminate the chart so that it can be used repeatedly.) After sharing information about a topic or book, students ask each other questions that begin with one of the investigative words at the top of the chart. After a question has been posed and answered, the child who posed the question writes her or his name at the bottom of the column for that investigative word. Listing the names on the chart recognizes students for their participation and rewards positive learning behaviors.

By design, a Question Chart encourages students to ask different kinds of questions as they see which columns have shorter lists of names. The listings also provide opportunities for graphing the quantities of different questions.

Kingore, B. (2003). <u>Just What I Need</u>! Austin: Professional Associates Publishing.

NOTES

The chart can be used effectively in every content area. Continue working with the chart in multiple contents over several days, and then pause as a class to analyze the different kinds of questions that are most frequently used across the different classroom discussions. Consider using a different colored pen for each content area and then discussing which kinds of questions are most applicable to specific content areas.

STUDENTS AS PRODUCERS

Students are producers throughout the multiple applications of the Question Chart technique as they pose questions related to the topic of study and answer each other's questions. In addition to topic discussions, the technique is applicable to other learning situations.

Show and Tell. As a child shares a show-and-tell item, the other children respond with questions for that child using the investigative words.

Reports. Other children pose questions to the reporting student about her or his investigation.

Read Alouds. Children ask each other questions about the book that was read aloud to the class.

Guest Speakers. Students interact with the speaker by asking and charting questions.

Question Chart

Who	What	Where	When	Why	How
				Karl	
	Patrick			Matt W.	
	Katie		Hallie	Jeff	
	Nicole	Scott	Ruth	Anna	
Joan	Jessica	Amber	Nicholas	Piper	
Suzy	Jeff	Nicholas	Katie	Nicole	Jamie
Steve	Grechen	Tyler	Lin	Matt W.	Jim
Katie	Ron	Lin	Matt L.	Tyler	Steve
David	Piper	Jim	Grechen	Jeff	Lin
Jenson	Nicole	Sharon	Amber	Steve	Jenson
Anna	Steve	Brendon	Maria	Nicole	Lin
Sharon	Jessica	David	Steve	Ron	Marc
Tyler	Amber	Katie	Brendon	Nicholas	Piper
Jessica	Ron	Maria	Sharon	Matt W.	Grechen

Kingore, B. (2003). Just What I Need! Austin: Professional Associates Publishing.

Question Chart

Who	What	Where	When	Why	How

Kingore, B. (2003). Just What I Need! Austin: Professional Associates Publishing.

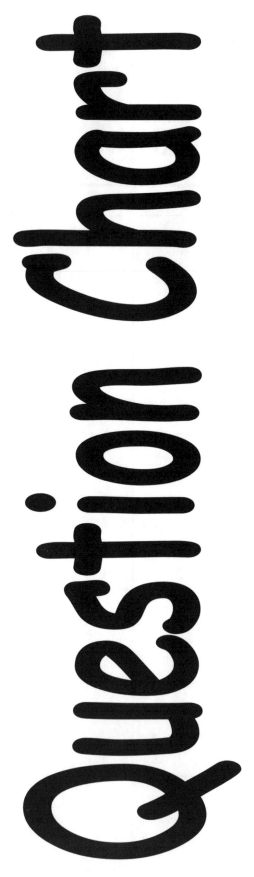

Quick Writes

PURPOSES

- To encourage students to analyze the most significant attributes or concepts of a topic
- To springboard discussions and more extensive writing about topics
- To review and organize information
- To assess students' high-level thinking and content integration
- To encourage and assess students' depth and complexity of information

GRADE LEVELS: 2 - 12

DESCRIPTION

Quick Writes challenge students to complete a quick response to a content question posed by the teacher. The responses are brief, factual, and serve to clarify or expand students' thinking as the students write to explain concepts or respond to ideas in their own words. Teachers have found that Quick Writes, another name for learning logs, provide a window into students' thinking processes and help point out areas or concepts that need more development.

Quick Writes may be completed in spiral notebooks or just papers stapled together with a construction paper cover. Some teachers add visual appeal by using shaped books for Quick Writes. (Even young students can draw a figure or shape of their choice, cut out multiple copies, and assemble their own books.) Encourage students to include art connections to personalize their Quick Writes books.

Provide two to five minutes for students to write a quick response to a question about the lesson. Questions, such as those on page 27, can be posed to begin a lesson, during a lesson, or as a closure task after instruction. The emphasis is on content depth and reflection rather than grammatical or mechanical correctness. If a student experiences difficulty developing a response, suggest that he/she just write thoughts or key words about the topic. Teachers and peers can respond to Quick Writes through verbal or written comments and encouragements.

Kingore, B. (2003). <u>Just What I Need</u>! Austin: Professional Associates Publishing.

Quick Writes can be used by any age of students to record key ideas, pose questions, make predictions, and relate personal connections to a lesson. They also allow students to summarize material, clarify concepts, concretely track their own progress with the topic, and generate ideas to focus class discussions. One second-grade teacher reports that Quick Writes are one of her favorite assessments. As her children complete Quick Writes for most of their thematic units, the writings show growth in fine motor skills, understanding of instruction, and written literacy development.

VALUES OF QUICK WRITES

* The process may be successfully used with any content area or topic.
* Students' active involvement and interaction increases.
* Students' analysis, synthesis, and reflection are required.
* Writing skills improve when integrated with any topic or content area.
* More learning modalities are incorporated.
* Teachers" increase their insights into students' perspectives and learning.
* Students can review content and concretely see their learning progress.

MODELING QUICK WRITES

With young children or students inexperienced in using Quick Writes, model Quick Writes with the whole group.
1. Use a pad of chart paper and record the children's responses.
2. Before, during, or after a lesson, provide a prompt about the topic for the class to discuss. Then, record their ideas on the chart paper to model responding to content and making personal connections to the content.
3. Review the content on the chart periodically as the topic continues.
4. As students become more comfortable with the process, provide a prompt and ask them to discuss their response in pairs for one minute before the whole class shares and the ideas are recorded on the chart.
5. Later, have students work in pairs and record their responses together.
6. Finally, have students proceed with individual Quick Writes.

QUICK WRITE VARIATIONS

Plan for flexibility and a variety of applications to increase students' long-term interest.
* Alternate using Quick Writes before, during, or after a lesson.
* Vary the time allotted for responses.
* Incorporate dialogue partners to respond to each other's Quick Writes.
* Alternate information-seeking with opinion responses.
* Assign different points of view.
* Encourage students to suggest questions to stimulate written responses.
* Encourage students to incorporate sketches and symbols.

Kingore, B. (2003). <u>Just What I Need</u>! Austin: Professional Associates Publishing.

QUICK WRITES:
QUESTIONS OR PROMPTS

TO BEGIN INSTRUCTION
What do you already know about this?

What questions do you have from your reading?

Write one key point from yesterday's lesson.

What is something important for you to know about this topic?

DURING INSTRUCTION
What do you think about this information?

How is this like _____?

What is a significant question you would ask? Why?

What do you think will happen next?

Identify a potential problem or issue.

AFTER INSTRUCTION
What is something important you learned today?

What do you think are the two most important points?

Write three things you would say to explain this to a younger child (or adult).

What did you do to participate today?

What would you like to know more about?

What did you enjoy and/or not enjoy about this discussion?

What is something you are doing to help yourself learn?

What is something you have accomplished since we began this topic?

What might _____ think about this idea/topic?

What do you not understand?

How could you use this to _____?

Kingore, B. (2003). <u>Just What I Need</u>! Austin: Professional Associates Publishing.

The Facetious Fictionary

PURPOSES

- To develop an in-depth understanding of word stems related to content vocabulary
- To encourage students' use of dictionaries
- To serve as springboards for vocabulary discussions among students
- To assess students' integration and transfer of vocabulary skills

GRADE LEVELS: 1 - 12

DESCRIPTION

The Facetious Fictionary is a humorous book of non-existent words created by combining prefixes and/or suffixes with a root word. Students create a fictionary word entry and then refer to a dictionary to document that the word is not listed. Instead of a more traditional definition, a fictionary incorporates scenarios of one to three sentences that use the word in an amusing context. The created words and scenarios are then combined into a Facetious Fictionary.

While a Facetious Fictionary is meant to be humorous, it motivates serious learning. To create entry words, students analyze the meaning of each word part. To understand the humor intended by another student's fictionary entry, students must apply the meaning of each root and affix. This process encourages students to master word stems in context and dramatically increases their vocabulary.

Inasmuch as 60% of all English words have Greek and Latin stems (CIERA, 2001), learning word stems is more powerful than learning one word at a time and targets the Latin-based language that pervades professional life (Thompson, 2001). When

3-19-22 Cinderella had to walk home from the ball. The <u>postvertment</u> of her coach into a pumpkin was just too uncomfortable.

Kingore, B. (2003). <u>Just What I Need</u>! Austin: Professional Associates Publishing.

children learn *tele,* they have learned a meaningful connection to *television, telecommunications, telemarketing* and dozens of other words that involve transmission over a distance.

Make fictionary content-specific by using roots and affixes related to a content area. Ask students to compare the roots and affixes most relevant to different contents or topics.

STUDENTS AS PRODUCERS

- Play fictionary as a game. Students use the Facetious Fictionary Words on the next page to create non-existent words. They then state their word code and challenge other students to pronounce and interpret the meaning of their word before they share the scenario.

- Entry words and scenarios for a Facetious Fictionary can be completed in centers, in pairs, or independently in vocabulary notebooks.

- To create an ongoing fictionary, students combine their fictionary entries into a notebook designated as the Facetious Fictionary or write each entry on index cards to file in a card box. Add visual appeal by encouraging students to illustrate the entries.

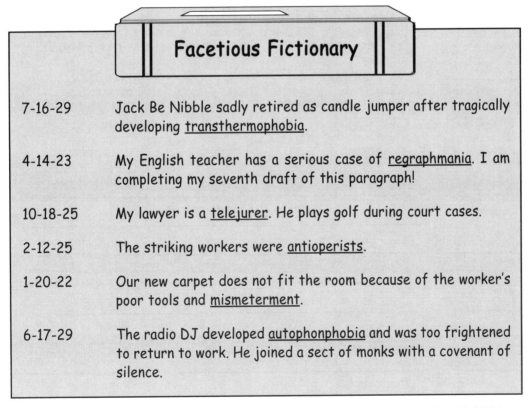

Facetious Fictionary

7-16-29	Jack Be Nibble sadly retired as candle jumper after tragically developing <u>transthermophobia</u>.
4-14-23	My English teacher has a serious case of <u>regraphmania</u>. I am completing my seventh draft of this paragraph!
10-18-25	My lawyer is a <u>telejurer</u>. He plays golf during court cases.
2-12-25	The striking workers were <u>antioperists</u>.
1-20-22	Our new carpet does not fit the room because of the worker's poor tools and <u>mismeterment</u>.
6-17-29	The radio DJ developed <u>autophonphobia</u> and was too frightened to return to work. He joined a sect of monks with a covenant of silence.

Kingore, B. (2003). <u>Just What I Need</u>! Austin: Professional Associates Publishing.

Facetious Fictionary Words

A fictionary is a book of non-existent words. Create a non-existent word by combining the following prefixes, roots, and suffixes. Use a dictionary to document that your word is not listed. Then, write a one, two, or three sentence scenario using your word in a humorous context. Combine the created words and scenarios into a Facetious Fictionary.

Word Code	Scenario
4-16-25	Benji dreaded the days after Thanksgiving. Since his mother is a dedicated <u>rethermist</u>, he knew there would be days and days of turkey leftovers.

Prefix	Root	Suffix
1. mis (wrong, lack of)	11. bene (good, well)	21. ness (quality)
2. anti (against, opposite)	12. op, oper (work)	22. ment (state of)
3. post (after)	13. hydro (water)	23. mania (madness for)
4. re (back, again)	14. graph (write)	24. ery (collectively)
5. co (with)	15. port (carry)	25. ist, er (one who)
6. auto (self)	16. therm (heat)	26. ism (condition of)
7. trans (across, over)	17. phon (sound, voice)	27. able, ible (able to, fit for)
8. bi (two, twice)	18. jur, jus (law)	28. itis (inflammation)
9. pre (before)	19. vert (turn)	29. phobia (fear of)
10. tele (distant, far)	20. meter (measure)	30. ion, tion (action or condition)

Word Code   **Scenario**

a. _____   _____

   _____

b. _____   _____

   _____

c. _____   _____

   _____

d. _____   _____

   _____

Kingore, B. (2003). <u>Just What I Need!</u> Austin: Professional Associates Publishing.

Homophone Tails and Echo Riddles

PURPOSES

- To use word plays as springboards for grammar and vocabulary discussions
- To encourage students' use of dictionaries and thesauruses
- To assess students' integration and transfer of vocabulary and spelling skills

GRADE LEVELS: 2 - 12

DESCRIPTION

Homophones are words pronounced the same but with different spellings and meanings, such as great/grate and to/two/too. In some regions of the country, words such as accept and except are pronounced very similarly and can cause confusion in usage. Extensive experiences using homophones in context is important for mastery. The humorous nature of Homophone Tails and Echo Riddles motivates students to want to spend more time working with homophones.

STUDENTS AS PRODUCERS

Provide students with a copy of the homophones on the next page. Model a few examples together, and then challenge students individually or in pairs to produce illustrated books of Homophone Tails and Echo Riddles.

Homophone Tails. Shel Silverstein's poem "Anteater" (in which the anteater actually is an aunt eater) and Fred Gwynne's books The King Who Rained and A Chocolate Moose for Dinner provide an amusing introduction to the humor of switching homophones in context. Students then create and illustrate "tails" in which they intentionally switch homophones for humorous effect.

My Deer Sister's Wedding
It was a grate wedding! Threw thee door came for bear-footed flour girls, followed buy a plane made of honor and ate attendance.

Echo Riddles. Echo riddles are riddles with pairs or trios of homophones for answers. Students skim the homophone page to select a homophone pair and then compose riddle statements that have that answer.

What does Queen Gwinevere say each evening to Sir Lancelot?   --Night-night, Knight
What did the boat owner see in the paper that excited him so much?   --Sail sale
What happened when the wind storm hit the blueberry patch?   --Blue blew
What was the result when Black Beauty caught a cold?   --Hoarse horse
What do you find in an empty abbey?   --None nun

Kingore, B. (2003). Just What I Need! Austin: Professional Associates Publishing.

Homophones

accept, except
acts, ax
affect, effect
aisle, I'll, isle
all ready, already
allowed, aloud
allude, elude
ant, aunt
ascent, assent
ate, eight
attendance, attendants

bare, bear
Barry, berry, bury
be, bee
beat, beet
been, bin
blew, blue
board, bored
born, borne
brake, break
by, buy, bye

capital, capitol
cell, sell
ceiling, sealing
cent, scent, sent
cereal, serial
chews, choose
chute, shoot
cite, sight, site
cue, queue

days, daze
dear, deer
dense, dents
desert, dessert

dew, due, do
die, dye
discreet, discrete
doe, dough

earn, urn
elicit, illicit
ewe, you
eye, I

fair, fare
find, fined
flea, flee
flew, flu, flue
flour, flower
for, fore, four
forth, fourth
foul, fowl

genes, jeans
gorilla, guerrilla
grays, graze
great, grate
groan, grown
guessed, guest

hair, hare
hall, haul
hay, hey
heal, heel, he'll
hear, here
heard, herd
hi, high
higher, hire
him, hymn
hoarse, horse
hole, whole
hour, our

inn, in
it's, its

knead, need
knew, new, gnu
knight, night
knot, not
know, no
knows, nose

lead, led
leased, least
lends, lens
lessen, lesson
loan, lone
lye, lie

made, maid
mail, male
Mary, marry, merry
meat, meet
mind, mined
missed, mist
mood, mooed

none, nun

oar, or, ore
oh, owe
one, won
overdo, overdue

paced, paste
pail, pale
pair, pear
passed, past
patience, patients
peace, piece
plain, plane
plum, plumb
pour, pore
presence, presents
principal, principle

rain, reign, rein
raise, rays, raze
read, red
right, rite, write
ring, wring
road, rode
role, roll
root, route
rose, rows

sail, sale
scene, seen
sea, see, sí
seam, seem
sew, so, sow
shoe, shoo
side, sighed
sighs, size
some, sum
son, sun
stair, stare
stationary, stationery
straight, strait

tacks, tax
tail, tale
tea, tee
their, there, they're
threw, through
throne, thrown
tic, tick
to, too, two

waist, waste
way, weigh
weak, week
we'd, weed
weather, whether
which, witch
who's, whose

your, you're

Kingore, B. (2003). Just What I Need! Austin: Professional Associates Publishing.

Sentence Cents

PURPOSES

- To serve as springboards for grammar and vocabulary discussions
- To encourage students' use of dictionaries and thesauruses
- To celebrate diversity in thinking by encouraging multiple correct responses at different levels of understanding
- To assess students' integration and transfer of skills including syntax, semantics, and writing conventions

GRADE LEVELS: 2 - 12

DESCRIPTION

Sentence Cents combines simple addition and grammar in an engaging learning task. Assign monetary values to different parts of speech, and challenge students to compose sentences that total a preset amount. While many combinations are always possible, students must understand the function of each part of speech to appropriately combine them into a meaningful sentence. Assigning monetary values to parts of speech adds an intriguing element to the learning task that motivates students to write multiple sentences. With this task, the practice of grammar can be fun.

The examples on pages 36 and 37 list some monetary values for sentence compositions. The example on page 36 is simpler and may be more appropriate when introducing the activity or when working with younger learners. The example on page 37 is more complex, as it incorporates different parts of speech to increase the challenge of the task.

PROCEDURE

Across the top of the chalkboard, on an overhead, or on chart paper, teachers write the part-of-speech categories they want to apply, such as nouns, verbs, conjunctions, adjectives, and adverbs. Students brainstorm words to list in each category and assign a monetary value to each category. Use an overhead transparency of the humorous sentences on page 35, or write a different

Kingore, B. (2003). Just What I Need! Austin: Professional Associates Publishing.

NOTES

list of sentences that relate to a topic of study. Together, use the assigned monetary values to determine the total value of one or more sentences on the list. After successful experiences, encourage individuals or pairs of students to determine the value of another sentence on the provided list.

Next, select some of the listed words. Model composing new sentences and then determining the monetary value of each sentence. Accent that all sentences must be meaningful. Provide examples of sentences that are contrived or run-on and contrast those with several examples of well-developed sentences. Later, as students write their examples, verbally recognize students who complete well-developed sentences.

STUDENTS AS PRODUCERS

Make a overhead transparency of pages 36 or 37, listing monetary values for the different parts of speech. Students individually write sentences for each value and then tackle the extreme sentence and the challenge task. This activity provides a valuable opportunity to assess students' transfer of skills in spelling, punctuation, capitalization, parts of speech, and sentence construction.

Topic Connections. Use Sentence Cents to compose sentences relating key ideas about the topic.

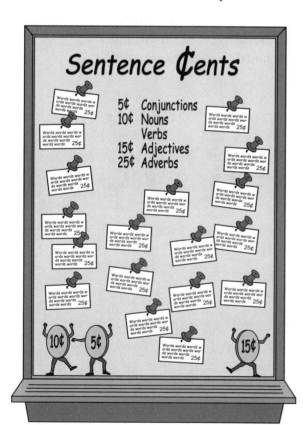

Vocabulary Development. Students incorporate the topic and content-related vocabulary in Sentence Cents sentences.

Bulletin Board. The teacher or a small group of students writes an example or uses information from one of the examples on pages 36 and 37 to create a bulletin board. Later, students post the sentences they develop. For each posted sentence, students include an explanation of the total for their sentences by listing the cost of each word used.

Kingore, B. (2003). Just What I Need! Austin: Professional Associates Publishing.

Sentence Cents
What's my value?

What do bumblebees do when they bumble?

_____ + _ +_____ + _ + __ + __ + ___ + _____ = _____

Clumsy the Clown collects colored crayons.

_____ +__ +_____ + _____ + _____ + _____ = _____

Jack and Jill moved to the flat plains.

_____ + _ + __ + _____ + _ + __ + __ + ____ = _____

The frog felt so jumpy, he went to the doctor.

___ + ___ + __ + _ + _____, + _ + ___ + _ + __ + _____

= _____

Do brown cows make chocolate milk?

_ + _____ + ___ + ___ + _____ + ___ = _____

Anteaters do not eat aunts.

_____ + _ + __ + __ + _____ = _____

Kingore, B. (2003). Just What I Need! Austin: Professional Associates Publishing.

Sentence Cents

5¢	Conjunctions
10¢	Nouns Verbs
15¢	Adjectives
25¢	Adverbs

1. Write a 35¢ sentence.
2. Write a 45¢ sentence.
3. Write a 50¢ sentence.
4. Write a 60¢ sentence.
5. Write a 75¢ sentence.

EXTREME SENTENCES
Write a sentence worth more than $1.00.
Explain its total by listing the cost
of each word you use.

CHALLENGE
What is the least expensive sentence
you can write? Write it, and explain its cost.

Kingore, B. (2003). <u>Just What I Need</u>! Austin: Professional Associates Publishing.

Sentence Cents

10¢	Plural nouns Helping verbs Adjectives Adverbs
15¢	Prepositions Pronouns
25¢	Irregular verbs

1. Write a 35¢ sentence.
2. Write a 40¢ sentence.
3. Write a 45¢ sentence.
4. Write a 60¢ sentence.
5. Write a 65¢ sentence.
6. Write a 80¢ sentence.

EXTREME SENTENCES

Write a sentence worth more than $1.25.
Explain its total by listing the cost
of each word you use.

CHALLENGE

Write a brief scenario. Include a 25¢ sentence.
How much does your entire scenario cost?

Kingore, B. (2003). <u>Just What I Need</u>! Austin: Professional Associates Publishing.

Word Analysis Chart

PURPOSES

- To develop an in-depth understanding of content-related vocabulary
- To assess students' integration and transfer of vocabulary skills
- To encourage students to organize and structure information in a comparative form
- To encourage students' use of dictionaries and thesauruses
- To serve as springboards for vocabulary discussions among students

GRADE LEVELS: 3-12

DESCRIPTION

A Word Analysis Chart is a graphic organizer designed to encourage students to analyze and compare the significant characteristics of several words used in the fiction or nonfiction text they are reading. Adapted from the linguistic study of semantic features analysis (Pittelman,1991), it also serves as an effective vehicle to revisit word analysis skills and check for understanding.

As this example illustrates, vocabulary words are listed in the left column, and the characteristics by which to analyze the words are listed across the top. The intent is for students to discuss and complete the chart.

Word Analysis Chart

SOURCE OF THE WORDS **Mouse and the Motorcycle**   AUTHOR **Beverly Cleary**

CHARACTERISTICS

WORDS	Part of speech	Synonym	Number of syllables	Long vowels	Suffix
momentum	noun	?	3	o	?
remorseful	adjective	sorry	3	e	ful
muttered	verb	mumbled	2	none	ed
astounded	verb	amazed	3	none	ed
incredulous	adjective	disbelieving	4	u	ous

Kingore, B. (2003). Just What I Need! Austin: Professional Associates Publishing.

NOTES

Use content-specific vocabulary that the teacher has selected to model the activity with the class or a small group of students. Or, to increase students' ownership, have them collect significant words from the text as they read, record those words, and analyze the words according to each characteristic listed on the chart. After completing one or more examples with the teacher's guidance, pairs or small groups can work together to complete the chart. Allow students to place a question mark in any box for which they are uncertain or for which the characteristic does not seem to apply. Discuss the similarities, differences, and question marks recorded on completed graphics.

The Word Analysis Chart is an effective tool in a foreign language or ESL class. Students use the chart to analyze the function and construction of new vocabulary terms. As a variation for greater comparison depth, students complete two charts for the same words--one in English and one in their other language.

Word Analysis Chart

SOURCE OF THE WORDS __Vocabulary list_____ AUTHOR _____

CHARACTERISTICS

WORDS	Parte del Lenguaje	Sinónimo	Número de Sílabas	Género	Afijos
casas	substantivo	hogar	2	femenine	s
creado	verbo	formado	2	no	ado

Translated by :
Advanced Academic Service, Grand Prairie ISD
Advanced Academic Service, Carrollton-Farmers Branch ISD

STUDENTS AS PRODUCERS

• Pairs of students select and list their choices of interesting words to analyze from the text or story they are reading. When they have completed the Word Analysis Chart, encourage them to meet with other students to compare the words they selected and their analysis of those words. Lively vocabulary discussions typically ensue.

• After modeling and completing successful learning experiences using the graphic with small groups of learners, some students want to complete the analysis chart independently. Students can also expand the graphic with different characteristics by which to compare words.

Kingore, B. (2003). Just What I Need! Austin: Professional Associates Publishing.

Word Analysis Chart

AUTHOR _____

SOURCE OF THE WORDS _____

CHARACTERISTICS

WORDS

Kingore, B. (2003). <u>Just What I Need</u>! Austin: Professional Associates Publishing.

Word Analysis Chart

SOURCE OF THE WORDS ―――――――――

AUTHOR ―――――

CHARACTERISTICS

WORDS	Part of speech	Synonym	Number of syllables	Long vowels	Affixes

Kingore, B. (2003). <u>Just What I Need</u>! Austin: Professional Associates Publishing.

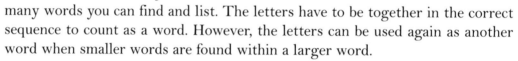

Word Hunts

NOTES

PURPOSE

- To mentally engage students in spelling and vocabulary skills
- To encourage students' use of dictionaries and thesauruses
- To serve as springboards for content discussions
- To apply visual techniques in spelling

GRADE LEVELS: 1 - 8

DESCRIPTION

A Word Hunt is a word play with great spelling applications. The spaces between the words are omitted, and the objective is to determine how many words you can find and list. The letters have to be together in the correct sequence to count as a word. However, the letters can be used again as another word when smaller words are found within a larger word.

It seems simple at first. But on careful inspection, it takes thoughtful analysis to find large numbers of words. For example, analyzing *DADDYYOU* results in a surprising number of words: *DAD, A, AD, ADD, DADDY, YOU*. Negotiate with the class to decide if words from languages other than English can be used. Determine if common nouns, proper nouns, or both are allowed. Including proper nouns and Spanish words adds *ADDY* and *YO* to the previous list.

Consider writing the entire Word Hunt in capital letters so the capitals do not signal where a proper noun begins. Model the first few words with the class to teach the process of the task. Also, negotiate with the students to decide if a word can be listed more than once.

Provide access to dictionaries. Students often want to skim a dictionary to brainstorm additional words and may also need a dictionary to confirm their "found" word is spelled accurately.

Make an overhead transparency of page 46, or develop an original Word Hunt. Present a Word Hunt, and allow students to work in pairs for a set amount of time to see how many words they can list. Come back together as a class to share results. If a word is disputed, ask the student(s) to produce a published example where that word is used. A dictionary is not the only resource students use to defend their lists.

Kingore, B. (2003). <u>Just What I Need</u>! Austin: Professional Associates Publishing.

To encourage students to persevere, set a challenge number for the number of words to attempt to find in the task. A challenge number is high enough to present a challenge but low enough to be beaten. For example, in the second grade spelling example below, the student set the challenge number at 16 when there are actually at least 31 words in the hunt.

When using page 46, focus on one Word Hunt a day for students to decipher. Lists of found words for each of the five Word Hunts follow on pages 44-45.

APPLICATIONS

*   Spelling words
*   High-frequency words
*   Vocabulary words related to a topic or story
*   Compound words
*   A Word Hunt using a quotation or a state motto

STUDENTS AS PRODUCERS

The following example is a Word Hunt created by a second grade student using spelling words.

SPEAKSWIMPORTANTOEACHEVENOFREEATUBEANSUNNYES

CHALLENGE: There are at least 7 spelling words and 9 other other words.

WORD LIST: 31 found words
speak, speaks, peak, peaks, a, swim, I, wimp, important, port, or, tan, an, ant, to, toe, each, even, no, of, free, eat, at, tube, tub, be, bean, an, sun, sunny, yes

---

*   Creating Word Hunts using high-frequency words, vocabulary words, or spelling words is an effective task to help students master those words. Since students enjoy the hunts, they typically spend more time on task. The activity is particularly applicable to visual learners as they see the correct letters of the words in sequence.

*   When appropriate, encourage students to prepare their own Word Hunts for others to work. Students can create Word Hunts related to the vocabulary in a current topic of study, spelling words, vocabulary development words, or the words in the class novel or story they are reading.

*   Provide students with copies of the 125 Most Common High-Frequency Words on page 47 to analyze and select words for Word Hunts. Or, have stu-

dents select seven or eight of their spelling words to arrange into a hunt. Students typically are thoughtful and analytical in planning the most productive words to use and how to arrange them for greatest effect. Working in pairs is effective as students can discuss combinations and piggyback on each others' ideas. Students enjoy the challenge of determining whose word list produces the largest number of words.

Procedure
1. Select the words for your Word Hunt.
2. Analyze the best sequence of the words to produce a substantial number of "found" words.
3. Write the list using only capital letters and without spaces.
4. As words are pushed together, double letters may occur. Determine whether leaving the double letters or dropping one will allow more spelling combinations. For example, as one fourth grader pointed out, dropping the double *Y* in *DADDYYOU* adds *DADDY-O* to the "found" list.
5. Make a list of all the words found in the Word Hunt. This serves as the answer key when others complete the hunt.
6. Add a challenge number to your list based upon how many words you found.
7. Switch lists with other students, and work their Word Hunts.

A Word Hunt for Compound Words

OUTSIDEDOWNTOWNSIDEWALK

CHALLENGE: There are at least 9 words in this word hunt.

WORD LIST: 19 found words
out, outside, side, sided, Sid, I, ID, do, down, ow, own, to, tow, town, towns, dew, walk, a, Al

A Word Hunt for High-Frequency Words

HEREDOWNOWILLOOKINDON'THATHISOFFROMYOUPLAY

CHALLENGE: There are at least 18 words in this word hunt.

WORD LIST: 36 found words
here, he, her, red, redo, do, down, ow, own, no, now, will, ill, look, OK, kind, in, Don, don't, on, that, hat, at, this, his, is, so, of, off, from, ROM, my, you, up, play, lay

A Word Hunt for High-Frequency Words

ABOUTHATWOULDIDAYOURUNOWHEREDONELIKEEPEOPLE

CHALLENGE: There are at least 20 words in this word hunt.

WORD LIST: 36 found words
a, about, bout, out, that, hat, at, would, did, I, day, ay, you, our, run, no, now, nowhere, ow, where, he, her, here, red, redo, Ed, do, Don, done, on, one, Eli, like, Ike, keep, people

A Word Hunt for High-Frequency Words

MOTHERESAIDOWNBECAUSEEDIDAFTERANDLONGOING

CHALLENGE: There are at least 20 words in this word hunt.

WORD LIST: 36 found words
moth, mother, other, the, there, her, here, said, a, I, aid, ID, do, down, ow, own, be, because, cause, use, see, seed, Ed, did, daft, aft, after, rand, ran, an, and, long, on, go, going, in

A Word Hunt for A Quotation

HITCHYOURWAGONTOASTAR.

--RALPHWALDOEMERSON

CHALLENGE: There are at least 15 words in this word hunt.

WORD LIST: 27 found words
hit, hitch, it, itch, itchy, yo, you, your, our, wag, wagon, go, on, onto, to, toast, a, star, tar, Ralph, Al, Waldo, do, doe, Emerson, me, son

Kingore, B. (2003). Just What I Need! Austin: Professional Associates Publishing.

WORD HUNT

CHALLENGE: *How many words can be found?*

OUTSIDEDOWNTOWNSIDEWALK

There are at least 9 words in this word hunt.

HEREDOWNOWILLOOKINDON'THATHISOFFROMYOUPLAY

There are at least 18 words in this word hunt.

ABOUTHATWOULDIDAYOURUNOWHEREDONELIKEEPEOPLE

There are at least 20 words in this word hunt.

MOTHERESAIDOWNBECAUSEEDIDAFTERANDLONGOING

There are at least 20 words in this word hunt.

HITCHYOURWAGONTOASTAR.
—RALPHWALDOEMERSON

There are at least 15 words in this word hunt.

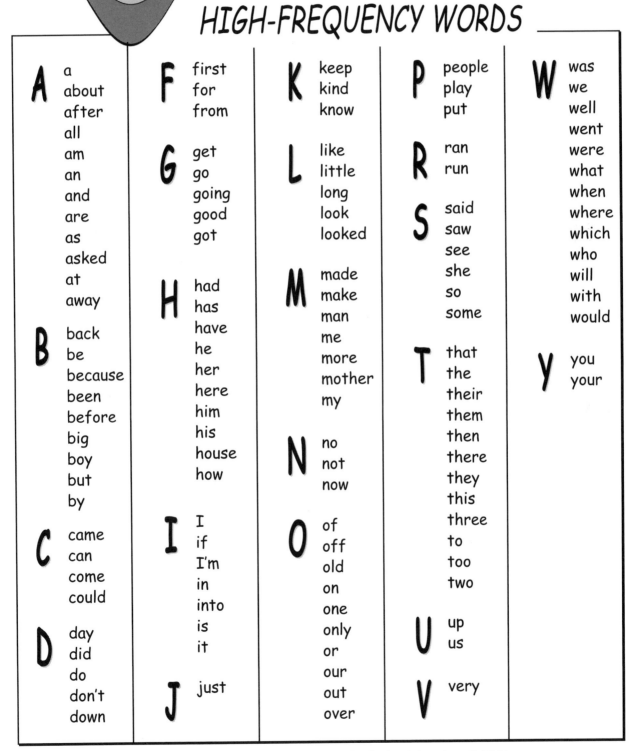

MOST COMMON HIGH-FREQUENCY WORDS

125

A
a
about
after
all
am
an
and
are
as
asked
at
away

B
back
be
because
been
before
big
boy
but
by

C
came
can
come
could

D
day
did
do
don't
down

F
first
for
from

G
get
go
going
good
got

H
had
has
have
he
her
here
him
his
house
how

I
I
if
I'm
in
into
is
it

J
just

K
keep
kind
know

L
like
little
long
look
looked

M
made
make
man
me
more
mother
my

N
no
not
now

O
of
off
old
on
one
only
or
our
out
over

P
people
play
put

R
ran
run

S
said
saw
see
she
so
some

T
that
the
their
them
then
there
they
this
three
to
too
two

U
up
us

V
very

W
was
we
well
went
were
what
when
where
which
who
will
with
would

Y
you
your

Kingore, B. (2003). <u>Just What I Need</u>! Austin: Professional Associates Publishing.

Word Map

PURPOSES

- To develop an in-depth understanding of content-related vocabulary
- To assess students' integration and transfer of vocabulary skills
- To serve as springboards for vocabulary discussions among students
- To encourage students' use of dictionaries and thesauruses

GRADE LEVELS: 3-12

DESCRIPTION

A Word Map requires students to organize an in-depth study of the vocabulary related to a topic or story. Word Maps encourage students to define and refine their understanding of the multiple applications of a word. These word investigations can be completed individually but are particularly effective when students work in pairs, encouraging conversations about the word.

Words analyzed on a Word Map should derive from the context of the fiction or nonfiction text students are reading. Provide dictionaries and thesauruses for students' reference, and plan a brief class discussion when pairs finish the map to compare their information. The maps can also be posted on a board or wall to invite students to read and think about the diverse responses.

STUDENTS AS PRODUCERS

- As a challenging variation, students complete a word map but do not reveal the word they are analyzing. They leave the word box blank and put a blank line instead of the intended word in their analogy and in the sentence they write that incorporates the word. Others review the map to try to deduce the word.

- Students develop original Word Maps that incorporate different attributes of a word, such as its root. These forms are then used by other students for their word investigations.

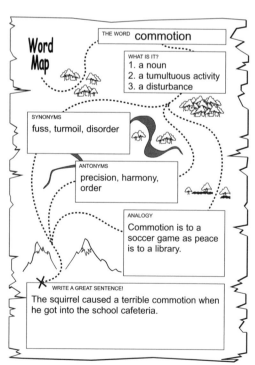

Word Map

THE WORD commotion

WHAT IS IT?
1. a noun
2. a tumultuous activity
3. a disturbance

SYNONYMS
fuss, turmoil, disorder

ANTONYMS
precision, harmony, order

ANALOGY
Commotion is to a soccer game as peace is to a library.

WRITE A GREAT SENTENCE!
The squirrel caused a terrible commotion when he got into the school cafeteria.

Kingore, B. (2003). <u>Just What I Need!</u> Austin: Professional Associates Publishing.

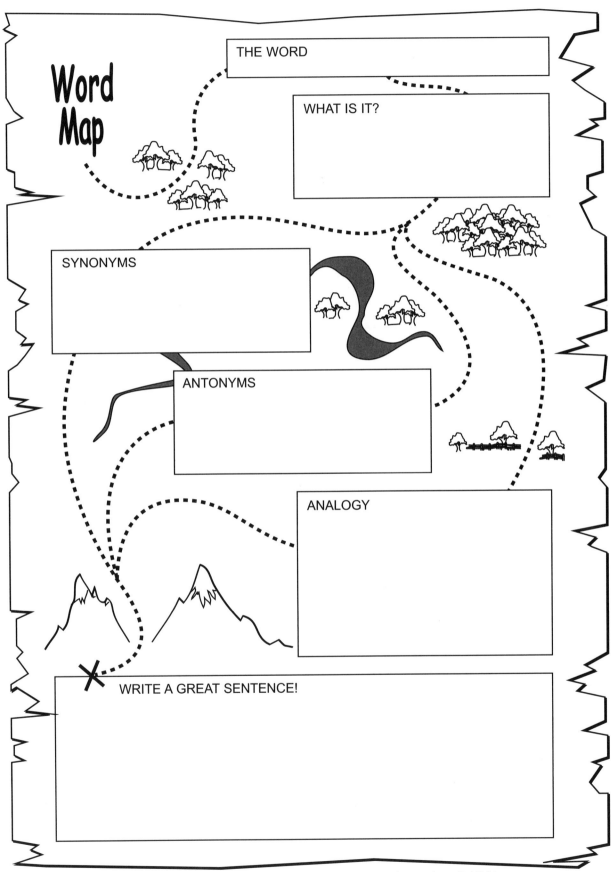

THE WORD

WHAT IS IT?

SYNONYMS

ANTONYMS

ANALOGY

WRITE A GREAT SENTENCE!

Kingore, B. (2003). <u>Just What I Need</u>! Austin: Professional Associates Publishing.

Analytical Cloze

NOTES

PURPOSES

- To encourage students to analyze and compare the significant attributes of a topic
- To integrate high-level thinking and content-related vocabulary
- To springboard discussions and more extensive research and writing about topics
- To assess students' vocabulary, topic information, and integration of skills
- To model summarization

GRADE LEVELS: 1 - 12

DESCRIPTION

Analytical Cloze is a procedure for analyzing the attributes or major characteristics of a topic. Students are shown a paragraph summarizing the key content of a topic but omitting a small number of words. The students' task is to fill in the missing words. The words most significant to the topic are omitted so that students must analyze context to determine which words to add to complete the paragraph. The process activates students' schema about the topic and focuses their discussions and further learning.

PROCEDURE

To introduce the process, make an overhead transparency of page 52. Cut apart the three examples, and select the most appropriate one to use to model Analytical Cloze.

1. Initially, students work individually for two minutes to fill one word in each blank. Challenge students to be prepared to explain a reason for their word choices.
2. Next, students form small groups to discuss and compare word choices. They can change any word they wish, but they must have a thoughtful reason for any change. This step requires three or four minutes.
3. Invite discussions and comparisons between groups or as a whole class.

The entire process takes less than ten minutes. It effectively involves students in analyzing the content the class is studying, and it is a strong closure activity. The process is also applicable before instruction to assess what

Kingore, B. (2003). *Just What I Need!* Austin: Professional Associates Publishing.

students already know about the topic and to motivate students to want to learn more.

   Consensus Building. After successful experiences with Analytical Cloze, inject consensus building as a variation that increases students' interaction. Each small group discusses individual choices and agrees upon one set of answers that represents the consensus of the entire group. Typically, discussion and negotiation become critical in completing this process and further serve to help students integrate information about the topic.

   Groups are then very curious about the results of others. If there is not enough class time to share among class members, simply post each group's word choices for other students and adults to read. Teachers report that students eagerly read the posted results and compare and contrast the different ideas.

   Examples. Three examples of Analytical Cloze paragraphs are on the next page. Suggested answers to those paragraphs are included here although the descriptive writing and fossil examples are more open-ended and invite multiple correct interpretations.

- Descriptive Writing: *extraordinary; perfectly; remarkable; cold; CEASED*
- The Formation of a Fossil: *flesh; Layers; presses; minerals; disintegrate*
- Procedure for Multiplying Two Fractions: *numerators; numerator; denominators; denominator; product*

STUDENTS AS PRODUCERS

- After successful experiences with the procedure, students can create original Analytical Cloze paragraphs that apply to multiple content areas and topics. The process is valued in elementary and secondary classrooms because it encourages students to generate key facts, examples, or attributes of a topic as it challenges an increased awareness of vocabulary selections.

- Analytical Cloze is an authentic opportunity to apply summary skills. Students create topic, book, or process summaries, plan three to five words to leave blank, and then challenge other students to complete their cloze example. Students want their summaries to be difficult for others. Hence, they spend more time reviewing the text and analyzing stronger content than if they were only completing a skill sheet.

- Analytical Cloze is an effective closure activity. Students can use the format when presenting their research or individual study to a student group.

Kingore, B. (2003). <u>Just What I Need</u>! Austin: Professional Associates Publishing.

ANALYTICAL CLOZE: Descriptive Writing

Fill in descriptive words to complete this scene adaptation from <u>Sylvester and the Magic Pebble</u>. Later, compare your description with William Steig's.

On a rainy Saturday during vacation Sylvester found a quite _____ pebble. It was flaming red, shiny, and _____ round, like a marble. As he was studying this _____ pebble, he began to shiver, probably from excitement, and the rain felt _____ on his back. "I wish it would stop raining," he said. To his great surprise the rain stopped. It didn't stop gradually as rains usually do. It _____.

✂ ---

ANALYTICAL CLOZE: The Formation of a Fossil

An animal dies in or near water. It is covered by mud and sand, and its _____ decays. _____ of mud and sand build up over millions of years. The weight of the top layers _____ the bottom layers into rock. Over time, the tiny holes in the bones fill with _____ and take the bones' shape as the bones _____. The bones are now fossils.

✂ ---

ANALYTICAL CLOZE: Multiplying Two Fractions

When multiplying two fractions, multiply the _____ of the two numbers together to obtain the _____ of the product. Next, multiply the _____ of the two numbers together to obtain the _____ of the product. Finally, it may be necessary to simplify the _____ by reducing it into lowest terms.

Kingore, B. (2003). <u>Just What I Need</u>! Austin: Professional Associates Publishing.

Bio Variations

PURPOSES

- To engage students in a simple activity that connects to a myriad of content areas and skills
- To review and organize information
- To springboard discussions and more extensive writing about topics
- To celebrate diversity in thinking by encouraging students to respond with multiple correct responses at different levels of understanding
- To assess students' integration and transfer of skills
- To engage visual and spatial learners

GRADE LEVELS: 1 - 12

DESCRIPTION

A Bio is a simple outline for writing. It presents guide words to prompt students' thinking about the content being studied. A Bio, like the content frames discussed later, is not meant to encourage a fill-in-the-blank mentality. Rather, it is a scaffold for thinking and fosters responses that are as varied as the students who write them.

The Bio, used in several sources, is traditionally presented as a Bio-poem, e.g., a short biography telling about someone's life. A form for that traditional version is provided on page 57. It is an effective device for organizing information about a famous person or historical figure. Students also enjoy writing a Bio for their own lives. Jessica's Bio on the next page is an example using the traditional format.

Customize the Bio by varying the guide words to focus on the information and skills most important in different content areas. For example, different parts of speech are easily incorporated as guide words. Main ideas, cause and effect, and analogies can be substituted for traditional lines or added as additional lines to elaborate the form.

Challenge students to use the character and a topic variation of the Bio shared on pages 58 and 59. Examples using the Topic Bio and the Character Bio are included on pages 55 and 56 to prompt thinking of other applications.

Kingore, B. (2003). Just What I Need! Austin: Professional Associates Publishing.

Jessica,
Friendly, nice, funny, first grader,
Related to Marty and Jackie,
Cares about Grandpa,
Feels hot,
Needs help in school,
Gives love,
Fears war,
Would like to see a kangaroo,
Lives in Marietta, Georgia,
Marsh.

STUDENTS AS PRODUCERS

Bio Riddles. Some students enjoy presenting a Bio to other students as a riddle. They develop a Bio for a person, character, or topic but leave the first line blank. After listening or reading the Bio, students try to decipher the missing information.

Bio Errors. As another variation, small groups of students complete a bio about a topic the class is studying but purposely include erroneous information. Others are to figure out and correct the errors.

Challenge able students to build upon the formats provided and construct original forms that focus on specific attributes of a topic or incorporate specific skill areas.

Character Bio

AUTHOR: _Traditional fairy tale_

TITLE: _Goldilocks and the Three Bears_

Character: _Goldilocks_

Four traits: _Young, lost, confident, selfish_

Three verbs with adverbs: _Hurriedly eating, carelessly breaking, foolishly sleeping_

Related to: _Daughter in a fairy tale_

Cares deeply about: _Satisfying her curiosity and personal needs_

Feels: _Alone, hungry, and sleepy_

Needs: _To be more thoughtful_

Causes: _A mess_

Fears: _The three bears_

Wants: _To see her own home again_

Resident of: _Imagination_

Simile: _She is like a pesky fly bothering others without purpose._

Main ideas: _Everyone's home should be respected._

Character Bio

AUTHOR: _Elizabeth George Speare_

TITLE: _The Witch of Blackbird Pond_

Character: _Kit_

Four traits: _She is young, lonely, scared, and foreign._

Three verbs with adverbs: _She warmly befriends, thoughtfully teaches, and aggressively comments._

Related to: _She is the granddaughter of an aristocrat from Barbados._

Cares deeply about: _It is important to her to help Hanna._

Feels: _She feels misunderstood._

Needs: _She needs to be loved and accepted._

Causes: _She makes others think and question._

Fears: _She is afraid of being executed._

Wants: _She wants acceptance of those who are different._

Resident of: _The story is historical fiction._

Simile: _She is like a light enabling others to see the need for change._

Main ideas: _It is important to have respect for people and for the differences among people without prejudices._

People are capable of changing.

Kingore, B. (2003). Just What I Need! Austin: Professional Associates Publishing.

Topic Bio

Topic: Quadrilateral

Four adjectives: Four-sided, geometric, shapely, straight

Five most important nouns: Parallelogram, rectangle, rhombus, square, and trapezoid

Related to: The patriarch of a very special family of polygons

Cares deeply about: Straight lines

Feels: The presence of angles

Needs: Its angles to total 360 degrees

Causes: Other polygons to respect its dominance in architecture

Fears: Others will find it "plane"

Resident of: Euclid's plane

Metaphor: Quadrilaterals are the box that architects try to think out of.

Major ideas: 1. A quadrilateral is a plane figure with four sides and four angles.

2. It has four straight lines.

3. It has six points of intersection.

Topic Bio

Topic: Skeletal system

Four adjectives: About 200, white, hard, growing

Five most important nouns: Cranium, spine, pelvis, rib, sternum

Related to: The muscular system

Cares deeply about: Organs

Feels: Ligaments

Needs: Calcium

Causes: Support and the shape of my body

Fears: Disease

Resident of: Aaron

Metaphor: My skeleton is a steel frame supporting my skyscraper.

Major ideas: 1. Humans have an endoskeleton.

2. Most bones are hollow with marrow cells inside.

3. The number of bones varies because some bones fuse at different times.

Kingore, B. (2003). Just What I Need! Austin: Professional Associates Publishing.

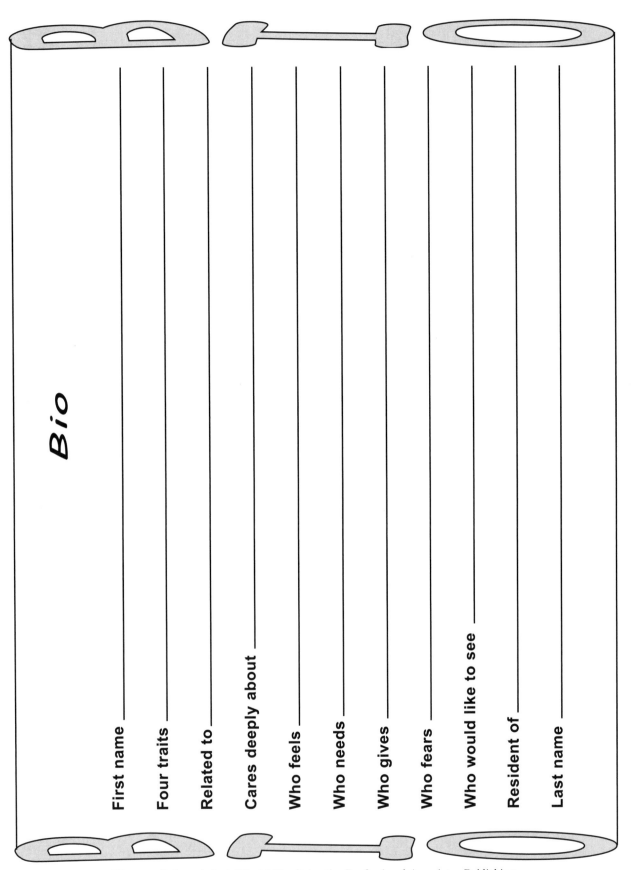

Bio

First name _____

Four traits _____

Related to _____

Cares deeply about _____

Who feels _____

Who needs _____

Who gives _____

Who fears _____

Who would like to see _____

Resident of _____

Last name _____

Kingore, B. (2003). <u>Just What I Need</u>! Austin: Professional Associates Publishing.

CHARACTER

Character Bio

AUTHOR: _____

TITLE: _____

Character: _____

Four traits: _____

Three verbs with adverbs: _____

Related to: _____

Cares deeply about: _____

Feels: _____

Needs: _____

Causes: _____

Fears: _____

Wants: _____

Resident of: _____

Simile: _____

Main ideas: _____

CHARACTER

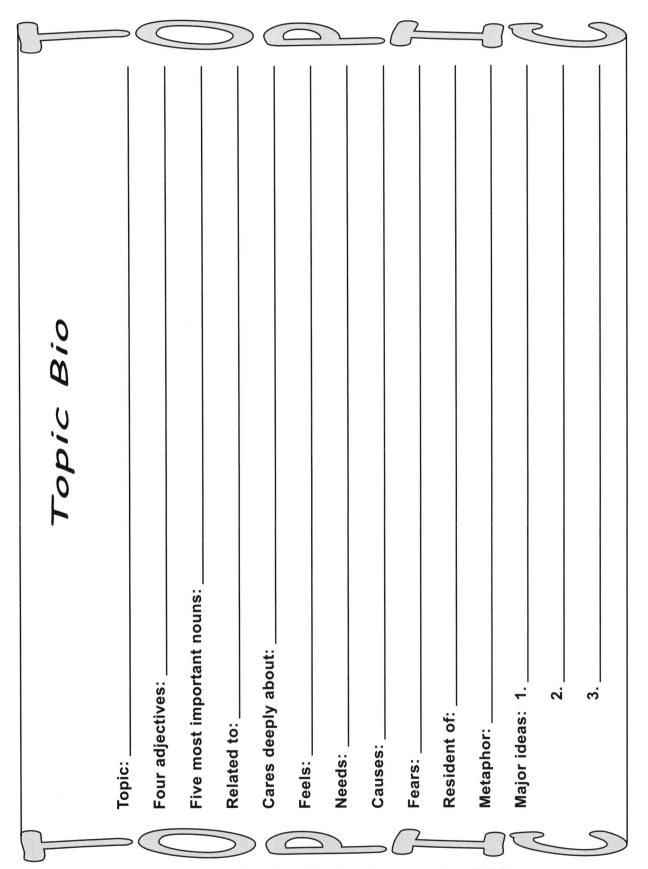

Topic Bio

Topic: _____

Four adjectives: _____

Five most important nouns: _____

Related to: _____

Cares deeply about: _____

Feels: _____

Needs: _____

Causes: _____

Fears: _____

Resident of: _____

Metaphor: _____

Major ideas: 1. _____

2. _____

3. _____

Kingore, B. (2003). <u>Just What I Need</u>! Austin: Professional Associates Publishing.

Content Frames

NOTES

PURPOSES

- To increase students' active involvement in content review and summarization
- To serve as springboards for discussing information related to a topic of study
- To enable teachers to encourage and assess students' depth and complexity of information
- To engage visual learners

GRADE LEVELS: 2 - 12

DESCRIPTION

Content Frames provide a basic outline that guides students' organization of information as they reconstruct the most significant content related to an event, person, or topic. Effectively used, these frames illustrate the depth of information and the relationship of the ideas or concepts under consideration.

A Content Frame is a series of sentence stems challenging students to write sentences that complete each idea. While the frames appear to be simple, they invite diverse responses and can reveal multiple layers of understanding. Like the Bio, they are not meant to encourage a fill-in-the-blank mentality. Rather, Content Frames are intended to be scaffolds for thinking that allow the responses to be as varied as the students who write them.

Initially, introduce the process of using Content Frames as a teacher-directed activity. Specifically, students need assistance and practice in learning how to identify the important pieces of information and the relationships among the facts. Deciding what information is important and how to organize the data is a vital process that requires active involvement, increases learning, and helps students construct meaning. After successful learning experiences, students can use and complete Content Frames without direct teacher instruction.

Several applications are possible.
- Complete a frame with teacher direction as a group consensus activity.
- A small group of students work together completing the frames to generate discussions about the event, person, or topic. When complete, different groups compare and contrast their results.

Kingore, B. (2003). <u>Just What I Need</u>! Austin: Professional Associates Publishing.

Event Frame

EVENT: _First man landing on the moon_

This event occurred _on July 20, 1969_
during _the Cold War space race_ .
The issue was _prestige and power. The US feared that the_
Soviet Union would dominate the Earth from space.

The most significant thing about this event is _that man could_
actually land on the moon
because _the required technological advancements and_
expenses seemed insurmountable .
The second most significant thing is _the information scientists_
learned about the moon
because _of the moon rock samples_

A person or place crucial in this event was _Neil Armstrong_
because _he took the first step on the moon and said: "That's_
one small step for man, one giant leap for mankind" .
The problem was resolved when _Apollo 11 and the astronauts_
safely returned home and the US celebrated its success .
If I had been involved in this event, _I would want to be the sci-_
entist who planned the after-launch procedures .
In my opinion, _this event illustrates man's ability to overcome_
complex issues when there is a need for change

- Students complete the frames individually to demonstrate their depth of content knowledge and comprehension.

STUDENTS AS PRODUCERS

- Challenge able students to build upon the provided Content Frames and construct their own original frames that focus on specific attributes.

- Encourage students sharing oral presentations or research to construct frames to use as a group closure activity.

Person Frame

PERSON: _Waterhouse Hawkins_

The most significant thing about this person is _that he built_
the first life-sized model of a dinosaur for people to see.

This person affected _paleontology_
because _he caused people and scientists to get more_
interested in dinosaurs .
Three main traits of this person are _creative_ ,
determined , and _brave_ .
These traits enabled this person to _make a life-sized model of_
an Iguanodon even though he was wrong about how it
really looked
An important person or place in this person's life is _Sydenham_
Park in London because _his model and several_
others are still there
Five words that best summarize this person are _sculptor, curiosi-_
ty, imagination, creator, and risk-taker
If I could interview this person, I would ask _what he said to_
those people to get them to eat dinner inside a dinosaur

In my opinion, _Mr. Hawkins helped all of us have a chance to_
learn about dinosaurs

Topic Frame

TOPIC: _Rain forests_

A significant point about this topic is _that rain forests include_
some of the most precious natural resources on Earth
.
Another important idea is _that 50% of the world's medicines_
are made from plants that only grow in the rain forests
.
Something interesting is _the animals that live there_
because _many grow so big. Some bats have wingspans of_
5.5 feet, and anacondas weigh over 500 pounds. .
Two key factors to remember are _that the forest gets at least_
80 inches of rain a year and _only 1% of the sunlight_
gets through to the forest floor .
                        Important people
An important person or place related to this topic is _are the_
indigenous people because _the forest has been_
their natural home for centuries .
Three words to remember about this topic are _life-providing_ ,
vital , and _endangered_ .
I relate this topic to _responsibility_
because _we are responsible for protecting the Earth for the_
future .
In my opinion, _the rain forest is the most interesting biome_

Kingore, B. (2003). <u>Just What I Need</u>! Austin: Professional Associates Publishing.

Event Frame

EVENT:_____

This event occurred _____

during _____.

The issue was _____

_____

_____.

The most significant thing about this event is _____

_____

because _____

_____.

The second most significant thing is _____

_____

because _____

_____.

A person or place crucial in this event was _____

because_____

_____.

The problem was resolved when _____

_____.

If I had been involved in this event,_____

_____.

In my opinion, _____

_____.

Kingore, B. (2003). <u>Just What I Need</u>! Austin: Professional Associates Publishing.

Person Frame

PERSON: _____

The most significant thing about this person is _____

_____

_____.

This person affected _____

because _____

_____.

Three main traits of this person are _____,

_____ , and _____.

These traits enabled this person to _____

_____

_____.

An important person or place in this person's life is _____

_____ because _____

_____.

Five words that best summarize this person are _____

_____.

If I could interview this person, I would ask _____

_____

_____.

In my opinion, _____

_____

_____.

Kingore, B. (2003). <u>Just What I Need</u>! Austin: Professional Associates Publishing.

Topic Frame

TOPIC: _____

A significant point about this topic is _____
_____
_____.

Another important idea is _____
_____
_____.

Something interesting is _____
because _____
_____.

Two key factors to remember are _____
_____ and _____
_____.

An important person or place related to this topic is _____
_____ because _____
_____.

Three words to remember about this topic are _____,
_____ , and _____.

I relate this topic to _____
because _____
_____.

In my opinion, _____
_____.

Kingore, B. (2003). Just What I Need! Austin: Professional Associates Publishing.

Initial Sentences

PURPOSES

- To increase students' active involvement in content review and summarization
- To serve as springboards for discussing information related to a topic of study
- To enable teachers to encourage and assess students' depth and complexity of information
- To assess students' integration and transfer of skills including context clues, syntax, semantics, and writing conventions.
- To engage visual learners

GRADE LEVELS: K - 12

DESCRIPTION

Initial Sentences are sentences in which only the first letter of each word is shared. Students must analyze the initials in context to complete the sentence. It is an open-ended activity with a multitude of different possibilities for correct responses. For example **I l B** could be *I like Barbara, I loathe Buicks,* and *Iguanas love Bermuda.*

I like Barbara.
I loathe Buicks.
Iguanas love Bermuda.

Introduce the activity by writing on the board or overhead the initials of a simple, three-word sentence, such as the one in the previous paragraph. Students brainstorm and list as many different possible sentences as they can. Discuss the role of punctuation and capitalization as clues to the solution.

Model the activity several times to develop students' understanding of the process and objectives for the task. Move from shorter to longer sentences, and use examples that positively incorporate class experiences and students' names.

1. W g t l a 11:45.
   We go to lunch at 11:45.
2. Y, E a J p t r a DNA.
   Yesterday, Eric and Jamie presented their report about DNA.

Kingore, B. (2003). Just What I Need! Austin: Professional Associates Publishing.

NOTES
As soon as the students understand the process, begin using content-related Initial Sentences. Multiple content and skill applications are possible.

APPLICATIONS

Capitalization and Punctuation
* Develop sentences for each application of capitalization and punctuation that the class is learning.
  1. *M, S, a F h f S.*
     Marc, Sean, and Fredrick had fun Saturday.
  2. *A S, I p t r m.*
     After Saturday, I plan to read more.
     Aunt Sally, I pruned the red maple.

Cause and Effect
* Construct one or two sentences relating the cause and effect of an event.
  1. *A m e i 1906 r i a d f i S F.*
     A major earthquake in 1906 resulted in a devastating fire in San Francisco.
  2. *W H_2O i h t 100° C, i b a g.*
     When H_2O is heated to 100° Celsius, it becomes a gas.

Current Events
* Construct sentences for events, locations, and famous people in the news.
  W w t P d a t e a h c?
  What will the President do about the economy and health care?

Historical Event and Historical Figure
* Construct sentences for the key events during an historical era.
* Develop sentences that relate the most significant traits and/or events involving historical figures.
  1. *T C S o A s b t d w t p o t U.*
     The Confederate States of America seceded because they disagreed with the policies of the Union.
  2. *T J w a b i, a, a s.*
     Thomas Jefferson was a brilliant inventor, author, and statesman.

Main Ideas and Key Points
* As a closure activity, create one or more Initial Sentences that state the major ideas or most significant points of the lesson or discussion. Make an overhead transparency of page 69, and use it to write on and share with students to conclude the review of text.

Novel Response---Elements of Literature
* Create sentences for the setting, characters, problem, key events, solution,

Kingore, B. (2003). <u>Just What I Need</u>! Austin: Professional Associates Publishing.

and main ideas. (See the example on the next page based upon the book <u>The Yellow Star</u>.)

Process and Sequence
* Construct sentences that retell one or more steps in the sequence of a process or procedure.
  1. *T f s i t s m i c o.*
     The first step in the scientific method is careful observation.
  2. *T d t a o a c, m π t t r s.*
     To determine the area of a circle, multiply π times the radius squared.
* Develop a series of sentences to retell a story in sequence.

Spelling
* Create sentences using spelling words in context. Students have to more actively remember the spelling words as they figure out which is used in each sentence.
  T e o M F i 3776 m.
  The <u>elevation</u> of Mt. Fuji is 3776 meters.

Summary
* Develop sentences to retell the beginning, middle, and end of a story.
* Write two to four sentences that summarize a story, historical event, process, or topic.
  R a J w i l, b t f w a w. T t t t d t b t, b i t e, t l e o.
  Romeo and Juliet were in love, but their families were at war. They tried to trick death to be together, but in the end, they lost each other.

STUDENTS AS PRODUCERS

* As a closure activity, students create one or more Initial Sentences that state the major ideas or most significant points of the lesson or discussion. They use paper or an overhead transparency of page 69 to write the main idea or three important points as Initial Sentences for others to decipher.

* Students work in pairs or trios to create Initial Sentences about any topic of study. This process encourages students to review and discuss the concepts and skills as they plan their sentences for others to solve.
  a. Challenge students to develop a more complex sentence that incorporates the key ideas, concepts, and vocabulary of the content of a specific lesson.
  b. Challenge students to synthesize the key ideas, concepts, and vocabulary of the content of a specific topic by generating a summary in the form of a paragraph of Initial Sentences.

Kingore, B. (2003). <u>Just What I Need</u>! Austin: Professional Associates Publishing.

NOTES

- Provide blank transparency sheets cut into strips appropriately sized for students to write on. As a group completes their sentences, they copy the initials on a transparency strip. Then, use the overhead so that all of the class can see and participate in the solutions.

- Make overhead transparencies of *Thinking about a book...* (on page 70) or *Thinking about the sequence...* (on page 71). Cut them into strips so different groups of students complete parts of the whole page, or provide the whole page for individuals or groups to complete.

Initial Sentences
for The Yellow Star *by Carmen Agra Deedy*

SETTING
T s t p i D d W W II.
The story takes place in Denmark during World War II.

CHARACTER
K C X o D i d t p h p.
King Christian X of Denmark is determined to protect his people.

PROBLEM
N s o D a r a J t w a y s.
Nazis soldiers occupy Denmark and require all Jews to wear a yellow star.

SOLUTION
K C a e D w a y s s t J d n s o a d.
King Christian and every Dane wear a yellow star so the Jews do not stand out as different.

MAIN IDEA
C a c f o a i s a h r v.
Courage and concern for others are important shields against human rights violations.

Main Idea

_____

_____

_____

Points

1. _____

_____

2. _____

_____

3. _____

_____

Kingore, B. (2003). Just What I Need! Austin: Professional Associates Publishing.

Thinking about a book...

SETTING

_____

CHARACTER

_____

PROBLEM

_____

EVENT

_____

SOLUTION

_____

MAIN IDEA

_____

B O O K

Thinking about the sequence...

FIRST

_____

NEXT

_____

THEN

_____

AFTER THAT

_____

FINALLY

_____

Paper Tray Games

PURPOSES

- To engage students in a simple activity that connects to a myriad of content areas and skills
- To increase students' active involvement in skill applications
- To assess students' integration and transfer of skills
- To engage kinesthetic, visual, and spatial learners

GRADE LEVELS: K - 7

DESCRIPTION

Paper Tray Games* involve a game board (like the blank ones on pages 76 and 77) that students cut out and fold up the sides to make a paper tray. One or more scraps of paper are then wadded into small paper balls and dropped onto the board. Alphabet letters, numerals, words, or affixes can be written in the spaces on the game board, and a myriad of skills applied.

ALPHABET LETTERS
- Name each letter, or say each letter's sound.
- Write the letters in alphabetical order.
- Write a word that begins or ends with that letter.

NUMERALS/NUMBERS
- Name each numeral.
- Spell or write its number word.
- Tell which number is greater.
- Add, subtract, multiply, or divide the numbers.
- Make a fraction with the numbers, and tell if it is greater or less than one-half.

WORDS
- Use vocabulary or spelling words and pronounce each word.
- Compare and contrast the words.
- Use each word in a sentence.
- Place the words in alphabetical order.
- Write both words in one sentence in alphabetical order.

*Paper Tray Games evolved from an idea called Paper Wad Drop shared by Greta and Ted Rasmussen in <u>Smart Snips</u>.

Kingore, B. (2003). <u>Just What I Need</u>! Austin: Professional Associates Publishing.

- Write a word that rhymes.
- Write a synonym or antonym.

AFFIXES/ROOTS

- Explain if the affix is a prefix or suffix.
- Name a word that uses each affix or root.
- Explain what the affix or root means.
- Write a sentence using words that incorporate the root and affix selected.

Paper Tray Games are most effective for active participation and time on task when played individually or in pairs. The random nature of the game adds to its appeal.

Elaborated versions of the game are fun to develop. Three examples are shared: ABC Probability, the Number Sentences Game, and the Fractions Game.

ABC Probability

Show an overhead transparency of the ABC Probability Game Board on page 78 to the children. Discuss with the class what they notice about the board, e.g., it has mixed up alphabet letters, lower-case letters, and one missing letter.

Model using one or two paper wads, tossing them gently onto the tray, and marking on the Response Sheet (on page 79) each letter-box they fall into. Also, record each toss on the Response Sheet to determine the total number of times you drop the paper balls.

- Discuss what to do if the ball falls into the same letter-box a second time.
- Decide as a group what to do if the ball falls on a line between two letters.

After a few tosses and tallies, ask the class: How many tosses will it probably take to mark off all of the letters? Write the prediction on the Response Sheet, and explain to the children that everyone will fill in the actual number of tosses after completing the game.

Provide copies of the ABC Probability Game Board and Response Sheet to each student. Students record their predicted number of tosses. Then, they cut out the game board, fold up the sides of the tray, wad the number of paper balls the teacher indicates, and play the game. When the game is finished, students write the total number of tosses and analyze the reason for those results.

VARIATIONS:
- Name the letter's name and its sound before tallying.
- Say a word that begins or ends with the letter before tallying.
- Play the game using three paper wads, and predict how the results might change.

Kingore, B. (2003). Just What I Need! Austin: Professional Associates Publishing.

NOTES | **STUDENTS AS PRODUCERS**

- Students create new games by determining different data to write in the game board boxes.
- Student play and create new variations of the Number Sentences or Fractions games.

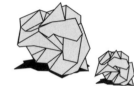

Number Sentences Paper Tray Game

Show a copy of the Number Sentences game board on page 80 with the 0 to 9 digits randomly written on it. Model using two small paper balls, tossing them gently onto the tray, stating an operation such as addition, and writing a number sentence using each digit-box they fall into.

- Discuss what to do if both balls fall into the same digit-box.
- Decide as a group what to do if the ball falls on a line between two digits.

Group students in pairs or individually to play the game. Provide each with a game board, and have each student wad two small paper balls for the game. Provide paper for students to write and complete the number sentences they create. For active involvement and increased skill practice when grouped in pairs, each person writes a copy of each equation.

Add a time element to increase on-task behaviors. For example, set a timer for three minutes and challenge students to see how many number sentences they can create and complete in that time.

VARIATIONS:
SIMPLER: Limit the board to a smaller range of digits, such as zero to five.
MORE COMPLEX:
- Use more difficult operations.
- Use three or four paper balls, and combine the digits into two-digit numbers before completing an equation.
- Use three paper balls, and create three-number equations.
- With older students, share a points system (such as those on page 81) before students play. After the first timed game, challenge students to compute their score and then play again to try to better that score. The accent is on personal best and growth rather than only recognizing the one student who achieves the highest score.

Fractions Paper Tray Game

Show a copy of a Paper Tray Game Board with fractions randomly written on it, such as the example on the next page. Model using two small

Kingore, B. (2003). <u>Just What I Need</u>! Austin: Professional Associates Publishing.

paper balls, tossing them gently onto the tray, stating an operation such as addition, and writing a number sentences using each fraction-box they fall into.

- Discuss what to do if both balls fall into the same fraction-box.
- Decide as a group what to do if a ball falls on a line between two fractions.
- For this game, the largest fraction is listed first in the equation. (Observe to assess which students can readily comprehend which fraction is larger.)
- The repeat space means to use the same fraction twice in a number sentence.

Group students in pairs or individually to play the game. Provide each with a blank game board, and have each student copy fractions onto it and wad two small paper balls for the game. Provide paper for students to write and complete the number sentences they create. For active involvement and increased skill practice when grouped in pairs, each person writes a copy of each equation.

Add a time limit to increase on-task behaviors. For example, set a timer for three to four minutes, and challenge students to see how many fraction number sentences they can create and complete in that time.

Variations:

SIMPLER: Limit the board to fractions with a common denominator.
MORE COMPLEX:

- Students use fractions that have mixed denominators.
- Students use three paper balls, and create three-fraction equations.
- With older students, share a points system (such as those on page 81) before students play. After the first timed game, challenge students to compute their score and then play again to try to better that score. The accent is on personal best and growth rather than only recognizing the one student who achieves the highest score.
- Students write fractions on a game board, exchange boards with another group, and play.

NOTES

Paper Tray Game Board					Paper Tray Game Board
$\frac{4}{5}$	$\frac{2}{3}$	$\frac{6}{7}$	$\frac{1}{3}$	$\frac{3}{4}$	
$\frac{1}{10}$	$\frac{1}{2}$	$\frac{2}{5}$	$\frac{1}{9}$	$\frac{1}{4}$	
$\frac{3}{4}$	$\frac{2}{7}$	Repeat	$\frac{3}{10}$	$\frac{1}{8}$	
$\frac{5}{8}$	$\frac{7}{10}$	$\frac{3}{6}$	$\frac{1}{5}$	$\frac{2}{3}$	
$\frac{3}{5}$	$\frac{1}{7}$	$\frac{1}{3}$	$\frac{3}{4}$	$\frac{5}{6}$	

Kingore, B. (2003). <u>Just What I Need</u>! Austin: Professional Associates Publishing.

Paper Tray Game Board

Paper Tray Game Board

Kingore, B. (2003). <u>Just What I Need</u>! Austin: Professional Associates Publishing.

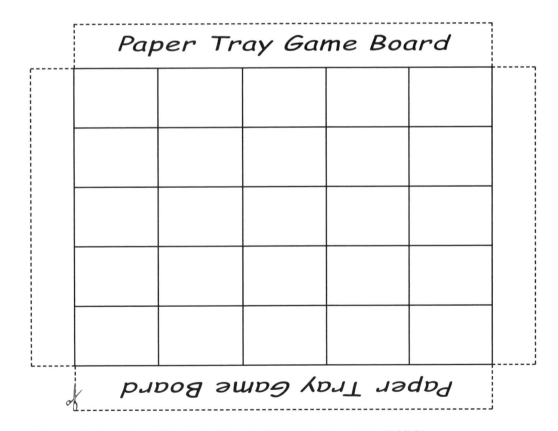

Kingore, B. (2003). <u>Just What I Need</u>! Austin: Professional Associates Publishing.

ABC Probability

m	b	a	u	l
r	g	f	x	s
n	w	t	y	d
j	p	e	q	o
h	v	i	c	k

Paper Tray Game Board

Paper Tray Game Board

ABC Probability

ABC Probability
Response Sheet

I will probably need _____ tosses.

Tally Marks

Number of tosses: _____

_____

A	B	C	D	E	F	G	H	I	J	K	L	M
N	O	P	Q	R	S	T	U	V	W	X	Y	Z Free

a	b	c	d	e	f	g	h	i	j	k	l	m
n	o	p	q	r	s	t	u	v	w	x	y	z Free

I actually needed _____ tosses because _____

_____

_____.

Kingore, B. (2003). <u>Just What I Need</u>! Austin: Professional Associates Publishing.

Number Sentences

3	7	4	8	0
4	2	1	6	3
9	5	8	7	1
4	6	2	0	9
1	7	3	5	2

Paper Tray Game Board

Paper Tray Game Board

Number Sentences

Kingore, B. (2003). Just What I Need! Austin: Professional Associates Publishing.

Number Sentences

CHALLENGE: How many number sentences can you create and complete in the time allotted?

Basic Points:

+10	Each number sentence that is completed
-20	Each incorrect number sentence

Bonus Points:

+ 5	Number sentences using subtraction
+10	Number sentences using multiplication
+15	Number sentences using division

Play again and try to beat your earlier score!

Kingore, B. (2003). Just What I Need! Austin: Professional Associates Publishing.

Fractions Game

CHALLENGE: How many fraction number sentences can you create and complete in the time allotted?

Basic Points:

+10	Each number sentence that is completed
-10	An improper fraction
-20	Each incorrect number sentence

Bonus Points:

+ 5	Each number sentence that has different denominators

Play again and try to beat your earlier score!

Kingore, B. (2003). Just What I Need! Austin: Professional Associates Publishing.

Paper Tray Game Board

Nouns

hero	intention	vaccine	laboratory	direction
theater	forest	sport	student	globe
solution	dictionary	realm	eagle	resource
school	idea	sculpture	problem	computer
memory	highway	cafe	asteroid	calendar

Nouns

Paper Tray Game Board

Use these game boards individually, or increase complexity by using both boards simultaneously. Drop one wadded paper ball in each tray, and write a sentence that uses both the selected noun and the verb.

Paper Tray Game Board

Verbs

relate	aggra-vate	predict	accent	agree
preserve	ponder	communi-cate	dance	thank
infer	scurry	seek	antici-pate	inspire
protest	under-stand	study	reflect	assist
address	teach	perform	listen	perceive

Verbs

Paper Tray Game Board

Kingore, B. (2003). Just What I Need! Austin: Professional Associates Publishing.

Paper Tray Game Board

Roots

audi	phil	vac	fix	tele
verb	scrib	bene	graph	astr
geo	fer	manu	log	ped
path	jur	dict	bio	op
metr	vid	phys	luc	ter

Paper Tray Game Board

Paper Tray Game Board

Affixes

pre	super	tri	co	ous
ist	a	phobia	anti	fore
bi	auto	hypo	tion	un
trans	re	ex	mania	dec
sub	ment	in	mono	post

Paper Tray Game Board

Use these game boards individually, or increase complexity by using both boards simultaneously. Drop one wadded paper ball in each tray, and try to use both selections in one word.

Kingore, B. (2003). Just What I Need! Austin: Professional Associates Publishing.

References

Center for the Improvement of Early Reading Achievement (CIERA). (2001). <u>Put reading first: The research building blocks for teaching children to read.</u> Jessup, MD: National Institute for Literacy at ED Pubs.

Cleary, B. (1965). <u>The Mouse and the Motorcycle</u>. New York: Dell.

Deedy, C. (2000). <u>The Yellow Star: The Legend of King Christian X of Denmark</u>. Atlanta: Peachtree.

Fountas, I. and Pinnell, G. (1996). <u>Guided Reading: Good First Teaching for All Children</u>. Portsmouth, NH: Heinemann.

Gwynne, F. (1976). <u>A Chocolate Moose for Dinner</u>. New York: Bantam, Doubleday, Dell.

Gwynne, F. (1970). <u>The King Who Rained</u>. New York: Prentice-Hall.

Ogle, D. (1986). KWL: A teaching model that develops active reading of expository text. <u>The Reading Teacher, 36</u>, 564-570.

Pittelman, S., Heimlich, J., Berglund, R., & French, M. (1991). <u>Semantic Feature Analysis</u>. Newark, Delaware: International Reading Association.

Rasmussen, G. and Rasmussen, T. (1993). <u>Smart Snips: Hands-On Thinking Adventures</u>. Stanwood, WA: Tin Man Press.

Silverstein, S. (1981). Anteater. <u>A Light in the Attic</u>. New York: Harper and Row.

Snowball, D. (1996). Learning high-frequency words. <u>Instructor</u>. September, 42-43.

Steig, W. (1969). <u>Sylvester and the Magic Pebble</u>. New York: Prentice-Hall.

Thompson, M. (2001). The verbal option: How can we challenge gifted students with classical literature, enriched vocabulary, and the study of grammar? <u>Understanding Our Gifted, 14</u>, 7-10.

Kingore, B. (2003). <u>Just What I Need!</u> Austin: Professional Associates Publishing.